Don't Tell Jim

Rose Leland

D1103794

Disclaimer

This book is meant to narrate one woman's subjective journey dealing with narcissistic abuse. This book is provided for personal and informational purposes only. This book is not to be construed as any attempt to either prescribe or practice psychiatry or other medicine. The writer of this book will use reasonable efforts to include up-to-date and accurate information on the Internet site, but make no representations, warranties, or assurances as to the accuracy, currency, or completeness of the information provided. The owners of this site shall not be liable for any damages or injury resulting from your access to, or inability to access, this Internet site, or from your reliance upon any information provided on this site. All rights reserved. No part of this publication may be reproduced, transmitted, transcribed, stored in a retrieval system, or translated into any language, in any form, by any means, without the written permission of the author.

Rose Leland

Copyright

Published by Pierucci Publishing

The Miracle of You. Copyright 2021, Pierucci Publishing

Introduction

Based on a true story, Scarlet Gaines is a struggling single mother of two teenagers who is by her mother's side during her battle with cancer. One week after her mother passed away, her stepfather of twenty-six years, disowns Scarlet and her children, and files a Civil lawsuit against her. This story is about abuse in a second marriage, betrayal of family, hypocrisy in the church, and the consequences of narcissism. A portion of the proceeds from the sale of this book will be donated to National Coalition Against Domestic Violence.

Based on a true story by Rose Leland

Don't Suffer in Silence

Please reach out to Rose on Instagram at

www.instagram.com/roselelandnc

On Facebook at https://www.facebook.com/Dont-Tell-Jim-105804251366222

Email us at RoseLelandNC@yahoo.com

Table of Contents

Chapter One: Happy Birthday

The alarm goes off and I immediately feel anxious and excited for this day. My sister and I have been planning this party for a year now. She reserved the Property Owners Beach House last July when her family was spending their usual summer months in Shell Island Resort in their second home; their home away from home she calls it. The community beach house is the perfect setting for mom's seventieth birthday celebration; the ocean front views, the sand dunes off the large back deck, huge glass windows touching the floor on the octagon shaped building. I am pretty certain I have invited everyone important to mom, hoping I didn't leave anyone out. Heidi Westin is the last-minute invite and I am not sure how she got missed for so long. Thank goodness Marin remembered her last week, and after searching the internet I discovered Westin Brothers Transportation had been sold in Raleigh a few years ago. I then reached out to Kate Mulvaney for help. Kate said she would contact some East Carolina University Chi Omega sorority sisters from the past to find out where Heidi is and try to get her phone number. Luckily, Kate called with Heidi's number, I apologized to Heidi for somehow overlooking her invite, and she said she would never miss mom's party, as mom is like a second mother to her from their Xerox days. She was planning to be at their vacation home in Shell Island anyway so how convenient it worked out.

Once I get out of the shower, I feel ready to take on the day, and I look at my husband still lounging in bed. Geez, I think to myself, it is almost ten o'clock and he has a lot to get done today and I feel aggravated he is procrastinating. Stan is in charge of the bar, so he needs to load up the banquet tables to set up on the deck, get ice for the coolers and the wine buckets and everything else. Since there would be so many church people from Seaside Baptist attending, and many of them non-drinkers, we are only going to provide beer and wine. Mom's sister June and her husband Wayne, and her older brother Johnny and his wife Sandy will be there, and they are the type of people that believe drinking is a sin along with these other church snobs. They all fit the Southern Baptist image with their judgmental attitudes about alcohol. Her younger brother Daniel isn't coming, but his son Miles just happens to be vacationing in the Wilmington area with his family this week so he can attend the party. Miles and Andrea and their two daughters live in the North Carolina Mountains and this is their first trip to Wrightsville Beach even though it's only five hours away. It is weird how my mom's family is not close, and I am not close to any of those cousins.

I decide I will do my errands now and go pick up the cake and arrive at the resort early for the four o'clock event. This should give me plenty of time to decorate and set up. I put on my Lily Pulitzer pink and green sundress which I have not been able to fit in for several years, like maybe five. Pushing my fiftieth year; motherhood, work and life stress has taken a toll on my body, but over the past few months, I started walking four miles a day, cut back on carbohydrates, reduced my alcohol intake, and the pounds are starting to fall off. I feel good and I am happy that I will look good in all the pictures I know will be posted on Facebook later in the afternoon and into the evening. After putting all the decorations in my car, and all the other utensils I think might be useful, I venture to Publix to pick up the sixteen balloons I ordered yesterday; eight purple and eight green, mom's favorite colors which she used throughout her house décor as well. It is a struggle fitting all of them in the back of my Honda CR-V but I am able to cram them all in somehow. There is a Liquor store is in the same shopping center and I decide to buy a bottle of Scotch for my husband and brother-in-law Rich to enjoy later after the party is over. The cake lady is located in the Sweetgrass neighborhood near the Wrightsville Beach connector, conveniently on the way to the resort, and in the same subdivision where our first home was built that we sold for financial reasons a decade earlier. Carolina Cake Queen also made my daughter Samantha's Sweet Sixteen birthday party cake, and the almond flavor with raspberry filing is one of the best things I ever ate. Once again, she has done a fabulous job with the purple and green golf theme cake and she also has made two dozen matching cupcakes with a golf trivet on each one.

Driving over the connector, I feel a calmness come over me as the car reaches the peak of the bridge and I admire the view of the picturesque Atlantic Ocean. It was nineteen ninety-one when I fell in love with this view, when I was working for USA TODAY and I remember that moment every time I see it. Little did I know back then when this bridge was built, that four years later I would leave my life in Charlotte and establish a future in Wilmington. The view today is just as special knowing all the eighty plus guests would soon be traveling over this structure to enter the quaint beach town to pass into the prestigious gated Shell Island resort.

The hot weather is mild for mid-July and fortunately, the humidity is unusually low. The heat will be tolerable throughout the day for the party. As I cruise through the back-gate entrance, having a property owner's barcode on my car is always convenient not having to go through the main security entrance, the anticipation is building in my mind. My love and devotion to family has always been important to me, but it was a trait passed down from my father's side of the family, and I carried it over with love for my mother, even though she has always claimed that she was a bad mom; that is her opinion of herself. She always tells me and Marin that she forgave my dad for the divorce, him having an affair with Darlene who he remarried right away. Mom claims that the reality is that if the two of them had gone off to college like they should have, they would have never gotten married, since they originally planned to go to different universities. My dad was supposed to go play football at University at North Carolina at Chapel Hill, and mom had planned to go to Lees McRae College in the Appalachian Mountains. Instead, they got married and stayed in Fayetteville.

As I drive down the long and curvy Oleander Drive, I get lost in my thoughts and I pass by the Property Owners Beach House and I turn around at the Legends Golf Course clubhouse to make my way back.

Being the first to arrive, I start unloading my car, then Marin pulls in the parking lot, and then Samantha comes right behind her. Samantha works at the Coastal Provisions restaurant in the Boardwalk Inn hotel inside the upscale resort, and she asked to get off early from her Hostess job so she could help with the party for her grandma, the only grandmother she has a relationship with since her paternal grandmother died when she was seven. She looks beautiful in her long blue and white striped maxi dress. The dress shows off her five feet eleven inches, tall, skinny frame. Although she is only six-teen she could easily pass for a young adult. It is no wonder she has older men hitting on her frequently in the restaurant bar, typical rich golf men on vacation.

Marin and Samantha help me get the rest of the stuff out of my car and we start decorating. I bought the decorations last week and I ordered the custom M&M's online months ago. The M&M's were expensive, but worth it as they were purple and green; some had 'Happy 70th' on one side and a golf-hole picture on the other, and some had 'Glenna' and a golf ball on the other side. We put purple tablecloths on every table and a large fake pink lily flower in the middle of each table with small green confetti around the flower.

Stan arrives next and he unloads the tables he took from our garage and other items necessary to use to set up the bar. Then Rich arrives with the boys. Larry and Bill are now seven and nine years old and I am hoping they will not get too bored at this adult event. They both dart off toward the beach to goof around like young boys do.

Swig and Swine Barbeque delivers all the food and they set it up banquet style. Marin took care of arranging the catering and she ordered barbeque with buns for sandwiches, coleslaw, baked beans, macaroni and cheese, and baked chicken. She also picked up appetizers from Whole Foods; veggie tray, fruit tray, and cheese tray so there was plenty of food. Now all the guests are starting to arrive, old Raleigh friends of mom's, church people, some of her friends from Northern Virginia, and Jim's daughter Sharon and her husband George and their two young adult girls: Leslie and Alicia. They traveled all the way from California. It is only their second trip to Wilmington to visit mom and Jim after they moved here to retire. Sharon and Jim have a strained relationship, and no one has ever been told the reason why, but when mom married Jim twenty-four years ago, she encouraged Jim to have a relationship with both Tony and Sharon as he was not close to either of them at the time. Tony drowned in a scuba diving accident in two thousand five. He was lobster diving with his best friend and friend's girlfriend off Coronado Island. He had lived in La Jolla, California. Sharon and Tony were raised mostly in New Mexico after Jim and his first wife Mary split, and their mom still lives there today. Sharon made Woodland Hills, California her home as an adult so both of

Jim's kids stayed close to each other since they both lived on the West Coast.

It appears most everyone is here now, socializing, drinking and snacking on the appetizers. Some of these people I have not seen in many years. Me and Marin are hugging many of them and thanking them for coming. Sheldon is the only important person missing, but he was away at church camp. Stan and I thought about driving two hours to pick him up early from Greenville University FUGE camp, but we decided that he has spent so much of his childhood playing travel baseball year-round, we agreed to let him stay at camp for the remainder of the week. Mom would understand, she knows Sheldon has focused on sports at an early age, and she knows the importance of athletics, considering she was voted Most Athletic Female during her Senior year at Fayetteville High School.

It's approaching five o'clock and I start looking out the side window along the front door. I see the black Lincoln Continental pull in the parking lot and Jim pulls in a vacant spot. Suddenly, I see a big white Mercedes cruise in and parks three spaces over and Heidi Westin gets out of that vehicle at the same time mom and Jim get out. 'Oh no', I start yelling frantically to everyone 'They are here, Mom and Jim are here, but Heidi got here late, at the same time, and Mom is going to figure it out and ruin the surprise. They all three are walking up the stairs together'! All the guests start to quiet down and stare towards the door. It opens and everyone yells 'Surprise'. Mom's look on her face appears to be one of surprise and excitement and she starts making the rounds hugging and talking to everyone.

People are eating and drinking and having a good time. We are taking lots of pictures and posting them on Facebook. Heidi and I talk about her late arrival and she said she told mom she was here for the weekend and decided to come to the Owners Happy Hour. That is the excuse Marin had given mom to get her to the party, that Shell Island is having a Happy Hour for Property Owners and Marin invited mom and Jim to attend. The resort frequently offers community type social functions, so it was a believable event.

Mom seems so thrilled and she tells us daughters 'Scarlet and Marin, you have outdone yourselves, what a nice party, thank you so much, I love you both'.

About ninety minutes into the party, we decide to cut the cake. It is on a table alone with the cupcakes surrounding it and I had bought golf printed cocktail napkins and small purple plates to stay with the color theme. After I cut about a dozen pieces, I clearly hear the Lord's voice whispering "It's a good thing all these people are here, because this will be her last celebration".

Chapter Two: D-I-V-O-R-C-E

The summer is coming to an end and my kids are back in school. Marin, Rich and the boys left last week although their schools in Westchester, New York don't resume until early September. As I drive down the interstate to work, I am trying to convince myself to call the tollfree number for the Employee Assistance Program. My marital troubles are starting to get the best of me. I am so tired of our financial troubles and the pressure that has been put on me during the past eighteen years. Stan was laid off from Guilford Mills in our second year of marriage and he has struggled to find another good professional job in this small coastal town. Then after Sheldon was born, he stayed at home and took care of both kids until Sheldon started kindergarten. Stan has worked odd part-time jobs since then. We've been struggling financially for years, and now my lifelong savings has been mostly depleted. We have downsized homes two times already and we are now in our third house; a two thousand square foot vinyl siding slab home; Vinyl Wasteland as one of my co-workers would say. There is nowhere else to downsize unless it would be moving to a condo or townhouse and I really want my kids to finish their high school years in this house. At least we are now living in the same housing development with Mom and Jim, so it is nice having them so close by.

As I pull in the parking lot on Leeds Avenue, I somberly get out of the car in the rain. I walk in the building and make my way to my office. Our new office building is sophisticated, and the overhead lights automatically turn on when you walk in my small office space, and then turns off when I walk out. I plop down in my desk chair, pull my wallet out of my purse, find my

United Healthcare insurance card and call the Employee Assistance Program number on the back. The lady that answered on the other end, asks what troubles I am having. I explain I want marriage counseling however my husband refuses to go with me. She asks for my zip code and then gives me a list of six counselors that are authorized to counsel me. I google them and visit their websites and I decide to go with Lisa Wilson. Her online form is easy to complete and she calls me right away to schedule an appointment next Tuesday. There is some relief inside me knowing I am finally going to have someone to talk to. All my marital issues and troubles I have kept to myself for a very long time.

Lisa's office is in a small one-story building with no receptionist. There is a small bell to ring on the entry way counter to let her know you have arrived for your appointment, as it is a shared office environment with a few other small businesses. Her counseling room is quiet, dark, and there is a big sophisticated baroque light blue chair I sit down in. As she greets me, I feel comfortable in her space. We talk about the insurance stuff first and I complete the new patient paperwork. Then I pour my heart out to her and it feels good to finally tell someone about my emotional pain and unhappiness I have endured for years now. At the end of the hour, we schedule my next visit one week from today.

The rest of the week is mundane, same ole' same ole; work, kids, long evening walks, etc. Looking forward to the weekend, mom had texted me already when I wake up on Saturday morning.

Mom: Let's go to lunch at Mosiac today. Pick you up 11:45.
Me: ok

Samantha is still in bed as she is tired from the first home volleyball match last night. This was her second year on the Varsity team; she was the only Freshman on Varsity last year and this year she is expected, and she is already getting more playing time. Stan and Sheldon left in the early morning around six to head to Greensboro for a baseball tournament. I piddle around the house, feed the dog, unload the dishwasher, shower and get dressed. Mom's gray Lexus pulls in the driveway and off we go for our usual Saturday adventure, whenever I was in town. The kid's sports tournaments were usually the only reason I wasn't available on a weekend.

'Do you want to sit outside?' and my immediate reaction is "no, it's too hot" as it is still the end of August and the humidity is still miserable. Mom has always been cold natured.

After we order our food, she says "Scarlet, don't tell Jim, but I want to buy Sheldon a queen size bed. He is getting too tall to keep sleeping on a twin bed. Let's go to Lester Brothers Furniture after we leave here and pick one out". Well, she is somewhat right as he is approaching six feet tall at age fourteen. Sometimes I feel guilty and incompetent having my mother buy me things and spend money on me and my kids. It makes me feel inferior since I am an adult and can't seem to provide for my family. Mom retired early from Xerox after seventeen years and she and Jim decided to move to Seagate, a suburb of Wilmington to be near me and my kids. They moved here in nineteen ninety-nine and mom decided to get her real estate license to keep working and Jim fully retired. She made over six figures at Xerox and she is very successful again selling real estate in this booming housing market along the Cape Fear River. But the money she spends on me and my kids is always a secret from Jim; Samantha's golf clubs, her private volleyball lessons, Sheldon's baseball bat that was three hundred dollars; a new couch for our family room to replace the ten-year old one we had that had holes in the upholstery.

We finish lunch quickly in about forty minutes. Mom doesn't eat much. She's been complaining for months about losing weight and feeling full easily. She's been to several different doctors and they tell her she's healthy.

Lester Brothers Furniture is a mile away from the restaurant. We sit and lay on several different mattresses before selecting the Sealy Posturepedic for seven hundred dollars on sale and the salesclerk schedules the delivery for Friday morning. On the way home my mind wonders to my counseling session and Lisa's word; "He took advantage of your kindness and your faith". Asking myself, how am I going to tell my parents, how am I going to tell my children, how am I going to tell my friends, and will I have the courage to tell Stan I want a divorce. Mom is rambling on about some church drama and the changes they are making with the worship services times and adding another contemporary service; attempting to attract new members, and how Jim is complaining about it. My thought is 'doesn't Jim complain about everything'.

Jim retired from Hewlett-Packard as an engineer where he worked for thirty-five years until they moved here. He was an engineer in the Army for ten years prior to his engineering career. He is the type of person that will never be happy, and everyone describes him as anal and difficult. Mom's church friend Lindsey once said, 'he must be difficult to live with' and mom replied to her 'I made a decision a long time ago to stay in the marriage'. Mom must have been referring to the time she separated from him briefly after one year of marriage. Mom rented an apartment, leased furniture and moved out of his northern Virginia home for one week. She moved back in

17

because he agreed to go to counseling. But Jim only went one time and I guess mom just decided to tolerate him because she didn't want to be divorced again. He was always correcting her and putting her down. It was stressful to be around them for a long length of time. Stan once said he can only handle being around them for a few hours as their constant bickering gets on his nerves. Mostly it was Jim just belittling her and everything she said, always trying to prove her wrong and him right. But mom is from that generation of women that believes everyone should be married. Sometimes I wonder how both me and Marin became so independent, and we both did not get married until age thirty-two.

Mom drops me off in the driveway and I then walk four miles around the neighborhood, and later watch college football on television the rest of the day. Stan and Sheldon aren't returning until tomorrow night and Samantha is spending the night with her friend Molly. I decide I am going to skip church tomorrow and enjoy my alone time at home.

Sunday morning my phone starts buzzing from the neighbors group text:

Patsy-driveway wine at 5 today.
Stella- gf why we gotta wait til 5
Julia-yea, weather is too pretty today, it's cooled off, let's do 4
Me-see you then, got us a bottle of prosecco

I am fortunate to have such good neighbors. We love to sit in a driveway in our beach chairs and sip wine. Most of the time we sit in Patsy's driveway but sometimes we will sit on Stella's back porch. We are all so different and in different age brackets, but we get along so well. Kevin and Patsy retired here to be near their three grandchildren that live in the same neighborhood, but their son and daughter-in-law live on the golf course in a different section, near Mom and Jim's house. There are ten different housing sections in the eight hundred homes of the Landfall development. Kevin retired from a public high school in Pittsburgh, Pennsylvania where he taught history and coached the boys wrestling team.

Patsy retired from being a Hospice nurse. Stella and Andy are in their late thirties with two elementary age boys close in age that are so well behaved and disciplined. Julia is divorced twice in her mid-forties and is a self-employed photographer that works from home. She never had children and her cats are her babies to her. We sit in the driveway for nearly two hours. Doug Hibben walks down the sidewalk with his dog not on a leash as usual, his big Bernese mountain dog that probably weighs eighty pounds. Stella asks, 'why does he thinks he is above the law'. I make a comment about him being a deacon in the church and maybe that is why he thinks he is better than others and he thinks he can get away with it. Julia states 'that is why I will never go to church, because of people like him'. We change the subject, and we continue to enjoy our wine time then we all go back to our homes for the dinner hour.

Monday morning arrives and all I can think about is my appointment tomorrow with Lisa. I leave work at five o'clock on the dot, come home and cook a chicken casserole for dinner, walk three miles and go to bed in the extra bedroom. Stan goes to bed super early since his part-time job requires him to be at a Home Depot store by seven. He is working for a vendor that stocks the tools and inventory at the national home improvement retailer, and he works a different store location every day. Sleeping in the extra bedroom for three months now, I use his early bedtime as an excuse to sleep alone, but the reality is I don't want to sleep in the same bed with him

19

anymore. I'm so looking forward to my counseling session tomorrow. My nightly prayers are: "I am sorry Lord I am going to be divorced". Then I hear Him comforting me 'it's okay, I am going to take care of you'. This inner peace comes over me, a peace that I have not felt in a very long time.

Tuesday morning, I ring the bell, Lisa comes out and I hurriedly walk back to her office suite and sit down in the comfy chair. 'I have made up my mind, I want a Divorce'.

"Marin, can I borrow twenty-five hundred dollars? I have decided I want to divorce Stan and I talked to Melissa, and she says I need an attorney, so I went to see one, and paid a two-hundred dollars consultation fee, but now I need at least twenty-five hundred for a retainer fee". Melissa is our cousin in Burlington that is a Divorce Attorney. She went back to law school after being an elementary teacher for five years. She is an Alumni for the first graduating law school class at Elon College. It is interesting how she explains the divorce laws are different in each state, and how the Judges are different in each county, which is why she informs me I need a local attorney. Lisa suggested I discuss my situation with Melissa before taking any action or before talking to anyone.

Marin responds by telling me that she is going to call her local friends here and ask him who the best attorney is in Wilmington and she is so generous, she insists that she will cover my legal fees. But I tell her I am also going to need help financially buying Stan out of the house. My life savings are gone, and I have no means to pay him off. Marin assures me not to worry; that I can borrow the money from her and pay her back later. But I won't be able to pay her off for years. The only way I will ever be able to repay her is by selling the house. She explains she will use her own money, that she doesn't need to ask Rich for any funds from his accounts nor their joint account. Marin doesn't need to work for financial reasons, but when Bill started kindergarten, she went back to work part-time at the local high school in the Guidance Department. She keeps her license active to practice psychology in both New York and North Carolina. Her husband Rich is extremely successful on Wall Street and he has been for years and he is frequently quoted in Forbes magazine and the Wall Street Journal. Darlene saw him on TV one day recently, on Bloomberg while she was channel surfing.

Several days later, Marin calls to tell me I need to use Robert Rosenfeld, that he is the best divorce attorney in the area. She asked several of her friends here in town and all three of them confirmed Robert is the best. So, I call the Rosenfeld Law Firm and make an appointment for Thursday. I feel so anxious, because I do not know how all this is going to work out. Maybe I should have paid more attention to my single friends and the conversations about their divorce settlements.

Thursday comes and I take off work at two o'clock to go downtown to River Street. It is an old historic former bank building that is probably three hundred years old but has been meticulously maintained. The atrium is huge with white marble flooring. I take the elevator to the second floor and tell the receptionist who I am. She offers me a glass of water in a real glass, and I sit in the wingback chair reading the Wilmington Star Magazine until Mr. Rosenfeld comes out and calls my name. I pay his eight hundred dollars consultation-fee with the check Marin sent to me via overnight mail. Then he says the total legal fees will be about five thousand dollars if there are no conflicts, no issues, and it is a simple, easy divorce. Marin is okay with that amount of money he recommends buying Stan out of the

21

house. My only hope is to stay in the house until Sheldon graduates from high school which is three and a half years away. At least now as a single mom, the kids will qualify for Medicaid since my income is low enough. My job as an Account Manager with Towers Perrin insurance agency in the Employee Benefits department pays forty-four thousand dollars annually. It will be tough making the mortgage and paying all the bills, but I will trust in the Lord to survive and I am confident He will take care of my needs. I will figure out a way to survive like I always have. Now comes the hard part; telling Stan I want a divorce, telling the children, and notifying all my family and friends that I am going to be a single mom.

■■■

Chapter 3: Fixer Upper

The kids are staying at Stan's this weekend and I am enjoying not being married and appreciating the alone time. They both seem to have handled the separation with ease and Samantha told mom she wasn't surprised, since I had been sleeping in the extra bedroom for months. His apartment is nice, and Sheldon has a friend that lives in the complex so he's got someone to hang out with. There is a community dock on Masonborough Creek on so they all can go fishing and crabbing. It's closer into town, near the Forden bridge, and it is convenient to restaurants and grocery stores like Whole Foods and Trader Joes. I took Samantha shopping right after Stan moved in and let her pick out a pretty comforter set and bathroom shower curtain and accessories. She chose a black and white theme with purple accents. My thoughts were that it would help perk her up about having to stay over there every other weekend and might help her adjust. Sheldon didn't seem to say much about the split, but boys are different, and he appears to be less emotional.

Last night I went out with my divorce diva crowd; or Crazy Single Mom Squad as Samantha calls it: Maureen, Melody, Margie and Bev. We like to go to BlueWater's Restaurant on Fridays and sit outside on the intracoastal waterway and it's the cheapest happy hour in town; four dollars for a glass of Pinot Grigio and half-priced appetizers. But we have to get there at precisely four o'clock to get a table because it gets so crowded so soon, and then when happy hour ends at seven, the place clears out within a half hour.

On Saturday morning my dog starts barking and she wakes me up around seven, which is late for me, and mom has already sent at text.

Want to go to lunch today?
Me: 'yea, pick me up at noon'.

The newspaper is wet from the storm last night, so I can't salvage it to read it. After I make a cup of coffee in the Keurig, I read the Wilmington Star online. Then I shower and get ready and watch HGTV until it is time to go.

"Where do you want to go today"? mom asks as I get in her car. "Let's go to Five Loaves".
It is crowded as always and instead of waiting for a table we decide to sit at the bar. I order the special salad and Mom orders the adult grilled cheese. "Don't tell Jim, but I want to remodel the kids' bathroom; it is so old and outdated and I don't want them to be embarrassed when they have friends over". My response is "Thanks mom, but it is not a need, everything is functional, the bathroom is fine like it is right now". Then she says 'You know, I've got that ten thousand dollars hidden in my underwear drawer, so I'm planning to use some from that stash of cash, and I know a contractor that did some work on house I listed for sale. Let's go to Lowe's next and look at bathroom vanities and tile for the floor'. Everyone but Jim knows about that ten thousand dollars mom has hidden in her drawer for years; me, Marin, mom's three siblings, her North Carolina and Virginia friends; Kate, Bethany, Cathy and Kathy, and her local church friends Lindsey, Libba, and Maryann. She has always said if she dies, we are to sneak the money out of the drawer without Jim's knowledge.

I finish every bite of my delicious lunch and mom barely touches her meal. She keeps losing weight and she keeps going from doctor to doctor trying to figure out if she is sick. She tells me she has an appointment with a new OB/GYN next week.

After lunch we head to Lowe's and I find a beautiful modern brown wood vanity with two drawers, a marble top, and space underneath for a large basket to hold folded towels and toiletries. Then we pick out eight-inch square tiles for the floor, a new white Kohler toilet, bronze oil rubbed faucet, chrome light fixture and towel rod, and the total damage at checkout is thirteen hundred dollars; that is after she gets a ten percent discount with her Military ID card, so that helps to bring down the cost. Mom tells me that she will have the contractor Josh call me soon to schedule a time to do the work.

We decide to stop at the Mayfaire Shopping Center and she wants to go to Chico's cause they are having a big sale. She tries on several pieces of clothing She asks if I see anything I want to try on and I say 'no'. I feel so guilty when she spends money on me and buys me things, and I am feeling guilty about her bathroom renovation plan. But then I see a necklace on sale for fifteen dollars, so she gets that for me along with the three items she tried on.

Josh calls on Sunday afternoon and schedules to come by tomorrow after work to look at the bathroom and the supplies mom purchased. He did some work for one of mom's clients before she listed the house in Sandpiper Pointe. Mom declares he does good work, and he is reasonable. He works for a local big builder during the day but does side jobs after hours.

He arrives on time at six o'clock and he likes the vanity and the color of tile I picked out and he says he can renovate the bathroom in one weekend. He would like to do the work the weekend after next, which will work since the kids will be with Stan, and I was thinking about going to visit my friend Ashley in Fayetteville anyway.

Mom calls just as I take the interstate exit off of interstate forty on the way back from Fayetteville. It is exactly a one-hour drive to my house from that exit. She went over to my house to pay Josh in cash and she says the bathroom is beautiful. She has already arranged to have Josh put down the pavers in the back of the house weekend after next, under the covered porch.
"I think I have enough money to remodel your downstairs bathroom next, and you need new carpet upstairs, then I want to remodel your master bathroom so start looking for supplies for all these projects". I am in awe that she intends to totally renovate and fix up my entire home.

Chapter Four: Diagnosis

"Dr. Rivers wants to remove my ovaries; she thinks that is what is causing my issues; losing weight, feeling full so easily, etc. She is going to schedule the procedure at Novant Regional Hospital and her office will call me soon with the surgery date. Dr. Rivers moved down here from Ohio last year and she spent a lot of time with me and reviewed my chart and all the tests I have had done during the past two years trying to figure out my problem". You can hear the relief in mom's voice. Over the past few years, I have lost count of the doctors she has seen and all the diagnostic tests she's had done; ultrasound, colonoscopy, CA-125 blood tests, etc. Mom has been paranoid she was dying. Last Christmas she gave Marin two thousand dollars to use for her fiftieth birthday celebration because mom didn't think she would be alive to see Marin turn fifty. Mom instructed Marin to 'don't tell Jim', as usual, because everything with mom spending money, always has to be a secret, even though she is the one working earning all the money. Me, mom, and Marin went to Las Vegas in November to celebrate my fiftieth birthday and mom's seventieth again, since it was still in the same calendar year as mom's birthday. But Mom told Jim that Marin treated us to that trip although mom paid for everything. We stayed in the prestigious Bellagio Hotel in a two-bedroom suite overlooking the famous fountains. The suite had two and a half bathrooms and there was a television in the bathroom mirror, that was a mirror only until you turned on the remote. It is the fanciest hotel I have ever stayed in.

The surgery is scheduled for Wednesday, June thirteenth so I request time off from work for the whole day. The hospital is across the highway from my neighborhood entrance and is within walking distance. I live in the second entrance of Landfall development off highway seventeen, but mom and Jim live closer to the first entrance. Jim picks me up from my house in his Lincoln and I hop in the back seat. It is still dark outside since it is six o'clock in the morning, and the weather is going to be beautiful all day. Mom is in the front seat, and she tells me that she is a little nervous. 'Why, this is a simple procedure, and you are now finally going to start feeling better'. She then says she has a bad feeling. I tell her that is ludicrous, but deep down I keep remembering the Lord's voice from her birthday party eleven months earlier.

All three of us go up to the second floor for the outpatient check-in counter. The Novant Hospital system is sophisticated as it has a palm print check-in for identification, and mom is a frequent patient in their facilities lately. Ten minutes later they take her back and Jim and I go downstairs and to eat breakfast in the café. My choice is the southwest breakfast wrap, and he gets bacon and eggs with cheese biscuits. The food is actually pretty good. Then we go back to the waiting area and watch the surgery progress on the mounted computer screen. It is color coded for the different levels of progress, purple for pre-op, yellow for in progress, green for recovery. G Reardon is now in yellow mode. We sit in the spacious lobby watching CNN on the large mounted television and I read through about three magazines and time is passing slow. It surprises me that Jim does not ask the lady at the desk to change the channel to Fox News since that is the station he usually prefers. Maybe he is just lost in his thoughts about mom. We have been sitting here for over an hour now and suddenly a male doctor walks through the double doors in scrubs and calls 'Reardon family'. Hmm, this is strange, who is this doctor? Jim waves him over. 'Hi, I am Dr. Neilson, a general surgeon on staff. Dr. Rivers has had a minor complication with Glenna's procedure. It appears the ovaries are attached to the colon and therefore, the ovaries could not be removed. We are going to admit her and prep her for colon surgery in the morning. This is a minor setback, and we are confident there is no cancer; just a growth that needs to be removed'. This doctor makes it sound simple and non-serious. Jim and I go back to visit with mom in the recovery room and she is calm as she is still slightly sedated. The hospital admits her and moves her to a room on the third floor. It is so nice outside still so I decide to walk back home and pack an overnight bag so I can spend the night in her room in the reclining chair. My office may be upset with me for taking an unexpected day off tomorrow, but they can get over it; my mom needs me. The colon surgery gets scheduled for two o'clock tomorrow.

The hospital is desolate at night as it is not a busy hospital to begin with. Most people in the north Seagate area of town only use this hospital for emergency room visits and minor surgical procedures. The hospital is not equipped to perform major surgeries. Another meal in the café for dinner is edible and I get the salad bar and a slice of pepperoni pizza. Mom is in good spirits and we watch Chopped on the Food Network for several hours.

The recliner chair is not comfortable, but I manage to sleep about five hours straight through. Since the surgery isn't until later in the day, I walk home to shower and I will drive back over when I am ready. As I finish blow drying my hair, I hear my cell phone ringing. It is mom calling, she must need me to bring her something on the way back over. 'Scarlet, I have ovarian cancer'. I am so confused because I clearly heard Dr. Neilson say yesterday that he was confident there was no cancer. 'What do you mean mom, that cannot be, the doctor said no cancer?'. She explains that they tested the fluid in her abdomen from yesterday's procedure and it is one hundred percent ovarian cancer.

Not caring how I look, I don't put on any make-up, put my hair in a ponytail, and quickly throw on some jeans and a T-shirt and dart back over to the hospital, in a rush to get back to her room.

Jim is sitting in the recliner, so I stand near the sink. Mom is crying, Jim is crying, and I just walk over and give her a big hug and try to refrain from crying. About five minutes later Dr. Neilson walks in and says he wants mom to go downtown now via ambulance to the main Hospital location to start chemotherapy today. His words make me feel like I am living in a dream, that this feeling isn't real.

I walk in the hallway, walk across the other side of the building, and I call Marin to tell her the news. I get her voice mail and leave a message for her to call me as soon as she can. Next, I call my dad. Crying on the phone, he says that the Lord has the power to heal her. But I tell him no, because the Lord already told me he was taking her, remembering how clear I heard His voice at her birthday party. I go back to mom's room and I try to compose myself as not being upset, trying to remain strong.

Several minutes later Dr. Rivers enters the room and says she is not sure mom has ovarian cancer. She thinks the cancer could be from the peritoneum. She explains the peritoneum is the lining of the abdominal cavity so the cancer would be outside the stomach, outside the ovaries, outside the colon. Dr. Rivers tells mom she doesn't need to rush into chemotherapy and that she will schedule mom an appointment with the OB/GYN Oncologist, Dr. Jenkins in the next few days. Mom is released now to go home.

Dr. Jenkins office is less than five miles from my office, so it is convenient, and I only need to miss about two hours of work or less. It's in the Monkey Junction part of town near another Novant hospital location.

Arriving before mom and Jim, I sit in the waiting area on the black leather couch. They arrive minutes later and mom checks-in with the young woman behind the glass window. Another lady calls her back shortly and tells me and Jim to sit in room number one, while mom gets examined by Dr. Jenkins in room number three. Over the past few days, I googled peritoneal cancer and printed out several information sheets. I give them to Jim for him to read while we wait. It is not good; everything read keeps playing in my mind; one hundred percent mortality rate, life span of twelve to twenty-four months after diagnosis, no cure.

Not sure where the idea comes from, but I decide to record the doctor on my iPhone so I can send the recording to mom's siblings and Marin so we all will hear the same thing. Mom walks in room one with Dr. Jenkins behind her. He introduces himself and then begins his speech; "This is nobody's fault, no one is to blame. You have seen six different doctors over the course of two years. This cancer is that difficult to diagnose. This cancer is that rare. I see over four hundred new patients each year, and twelve of them will have this cancer. Peritoneal Cancer is a form of Ovarian Cancer as the cancer cells look the same under a microscope. It is treated with the same chemotherapy drugs used for ovarian cancer. The treatment plan will be two initial rounds of chemotherapy, three weeks apart in hopes that the chemo will shrink the tumors. Then surgery will be necessary to remove the tumors, followed by four additional chemo treatments".

He says his nurse Lora will arrange the first round of chemo for next week and that his office staff will attempt to get the chemo approved in his office setting in lieu of having the treatments performed at the actual hospital.

Mom seems to handle the news with acceptance, as she has always said she would die from cancer one day. She never thought she would live a long life. And she has admitted lately she has had a premonition that she was dying. Dr. Jenkins leaves the room and then nurse Lora comes in. Lora is in her mid-fifties, pretty, with short jet-black hair. She has a calm personality, and she seems caring and nurturing. She explains to mom exactly how the chemo will be given to her and shows us the chemotherapy room down the hallway. Mom will be given anti-anxiety meds prior to the procedure to calm her, then she will be given the intravenous fusion, all while she is sitting in a comfortable recliner chair.

As the three of us walk out of the office and into the parking lot; we are all speechless. I say goodbye and I need to get back to work. As soon as I get in the car, I call Marin and give her the update. Her attitude is that cancer can be cured and with modern day technology mom can probably extend her life at least five years. Then I call mom's sister, June, whom I have not interacted much during the past twenty years, except when she and Wayne come down for their timeshare in Shell Island and she comes over to mom's house for dinner occasionally. June has the same attitude of Marin, so they are making me feel guilty for believing mom is going to die soon.

The next few days I go around telling everyone the news; texting, calling, emailing family, friends, neighbors, coworkers. One of my best friends in Charlotte, Karen, tells me her mom died from the same cancer fourteen years early. Surely, she says confidently, that there have been medical advances since then that could extend mom's life. But the reality is mom will be taking the same chemo drugs as her mom took, Carboplatin and Taxol. That is surprising the drugs haven't changed or improved in all those years. Karen's mom lived for eighteen months after her diagnosis. She sought treatment at Duke Medical Center in Durham, since where she lived in Whiteville, North Carolina was only a two-hour drive to the nationally known hospital.

Mom is already preparing for her hair to fall out and this is going to be interesting because she is somewhat vain. Lora told her it would start falling out after the twenty-first day of chemo. Marin decides to work on finding her the best wig available and she plans a wig party in two weeks at mom's house, inviting the church ladies and having lunch catered. Marin is not coming to Wilmington for the event, she just plans it and is going to pay for it.

I start thinking and planning in my mind how to live without mom. Considering I have never dealt with death much, this is not going to be easy. Then again, I guess it is never easy losing a parent or loved one. Both my grandmothers lived into their eighties, and all my aunt and uncles are still alive except one. Grief is something I have never really experienced.

■■■

The alarm goes off at six-thirty. Mom needs to be at the hospital at eight-thirty for the ten o'clock surgery. This gives me time to get ready, read the paper, make breakfast and get downtown by then. It was decided that I would spend the first two nights in the hospital and Marin would stay on Friday night when Rich flew back in from New York. It is convenient that her family was down here already for their annual summer vacation. Every year they arrive in Wrightsville Beach the end of June and they usually stay here until the end of August. Rich flies into town on Friday nights and then leaves again early on Monday mornings to work in Manhattan.

I don't sleep well, as I am worried about the surgery. Dad is coming to sit with us in the lobby to support me and Marin. Maybe he is worried mom may die today. Knowing mom's brother Johnny and sister June will be there too, I am concerned how June will react. June is the exact opposite of my mom; she talks a lot, and she is very opinionated. She still hates my dad today just as much as she did when mom and dad split thirty-five years ago. Not sure why Daniel isn't coming, but then again, those siblings are not very close.

There are so many people from the church that show up for support. Our hospital Concierge rep assigned to mom finds us a place on the second-floor atrium with about twenty chairs, overlooking the main lobby down below and with windows looking out over the front of the hospital. Me, Marin and Jim go back with mom to the pre-op area until they make us leave. Mom seems nervous, but who wouldn't be. Dr. Jenkins says he plans to remove about ninety tumors, and part of her colon.

Having the church people here is nice. They are mostly people from mom and Jim's Sunday school class, and everyone looks to be over the age of seventy years. Dad is sitting on the left side near Pastor Rick and Lindsey Lawton, and some man I don't recognize. June just keeps starring at my dad as she talks the ears off of Pearl and Rowland Levine. Maryann Caulder shows up at lunchtime with sandwiches, chips, and a cooler full of soft drinks. That sure is thoughtful, but isn't that what church people do for each other?

Finally, the nurse calls my cell phone to tell me the three of us can come back to the third floor waiting room and Dr. Jenkins will come speak with us. It has been over four hours now and he had said the procedure would be approximately three hours. In the back of my mind, I am thinking something is wrong; again.

We sit on a cushioned bench outside the waiting area because it's too crowded in there. Dr. Jenkins is in his scrubs, stands before us and says "The chemotherapy did not work like I had hoped. There was much more cancer than I suspected. I had to remove about three feet of her small intestine, six feet of her colon, and over one hundred of the tumors. I think I got all the cancer. She has lost a lot of blood and will be receiving blood transfusions. This has been a major operation and she will need to recover for weeks. With the surgery being more extensive than I originally anticipated, I do not want to give her chemotherapy again until she is fully recovered, at least six weeks from now, maybe longer".

Me, and Marin, and Jim all have gloomy looks on our faces. We don't ask any questions. We thank him and take the elevator back to where everyone is waiting. Marin repeats out loud what the doctor said, then everyone leaves the hospital except me, Marin, and Jim.

Mom wakes up in her assigned hospital room, and the three of us are here to comfort her. She seems disoriented, but that is expected with all the drugs she has been given. Marin and Jim leave about dinner time and me and mom are staring at the television.

She asks, 'Who all came from the church today?' I rattle off all the names, except for those people I didn't recognize. 'Was your dad there?' With a puzzled look on my face, because I didn't tell her he was coming, and I respond, "yes, he sat by Pastor Rick most of the time'. Mom explains, 'Don't tell Jim but I set up a private email account that I don't want him to know about. I am only checking it on my phone, so I can have some communication with others that Jim won't be able to see on our home computer. I emailed your dad last week, because I wasn't sure I was going to make it through this surgery. I told him how thankful I am that he has been a good father to you and Marin. And it makes me happy knowing his family is so close and they will be there for you and Marin and your families after I am gone. He replied back that he was coming today, to support you two girls. But I never told Jim, please don't tell Jim about my private email account, even after I am gone. And I want you and Marin to start using that email address also; golfgirl43@gmail.com

• •

Mom is not recovering so easily, and I am exhausted from spending five nights in the hospital, sleeping on the recliner that pulls out into somewhat of a small twin-size bed. It's been seven days and finally they tell the two of us early this morning that she can go home today. They will assign her a home health nurse to come to the house to help monitor her recovery. Jim gets there at ten o'clock and I decide to leave and go home to shower and will go over to their house later. I had to take off work, but I am determined to be by my mother's side. She texts me around noonish:

Mom: "We are leaving the hospital now"

Me: Ok, I will come over to the house when you get home.

It's two o'clock and I haven't heard from mom so I call her cell. "We just got home five minutes ago". Astonished, I ask "Didn't you get released from the hospital two hours ago?" not understanding why it would take them so long to get back to their home. 'Yes, but Jim needed to stop by Lowe's on the way home and do a few other errands. Walking through Lowe's was tiring for me, so I sat in the car when he went in Ace Hardware". Not believing he could be so inconsiderate, I just say "ok, I am on the way over, I am walking over now, see you in a few minutes.' Their house is on the golf course in the Heathland section of Landfall which is less than a mile from my home and I take the short route by walking up the cart path that leads to the back of their house.

Chapter Five: Holiday Spirit

This is my favorite time of year. I am always excited for both Thanksgiving and Christmas, and I make my usual plans to start decorating the house soon. All my friends make fun of me for decorating for Christmas the day after Thanksgiving. And this year I am wondering if it will the last Thanksgiving and Christmas I can share with my mother.

Mom: "Can we have Thanksgiving at your house? It will be easier on me because I won't have energy to set the table and it will be three days after chemo and that's always my worst day"

Me: Of course; I have already ordered all the food from Publix.

Mom: 'thanks, pick me up tomorrow at noon for lunch."

Mom's last Chemo is scheduled for Monday, and she seems to look thinner and weaker with each passing day. The home health care nurse Cindy will still be coming to the house as long as that service continues to be approved by her Medicare insurance. Mom likes Cindy; she's early thirties, single, and sweetly southern. Mom is fortunate that Medicare coverage has been approving every service and she is lucky to have continued chemo treatments in Dr. Jenkins office. It's convenient for me too since it's so close to my office and I only have to take off a few hours from work to sit with her. Jim always runs off to do errands during mom's treatment; because he doesn't get to Monkey Junction very often, so he patronizes stores that aren't located in the town of Seagate.

This is the umpteenth Saturday in a row I have spent with mom, every Saturday since her diagnosis. I guess in the back of my mind and in the back of her mind, we both know her Saturdays are numbered. But it is also my one free day of the week to get my chores done, since I go to church on Sundays as I volunteer in the nursery twice a month. Therefore, a lot of my chores are not getting done. It's basketball season, so Sheldon isn't home very much, and the yard still needs attention, mowing up the leaves, blowing off the driveway, trimming the hedges. Sheldon manages to help out some, but the weeding and pruning in my third of an acre yard is falling behind. My residential lot is the largest one on the street which is unusual for homes in a vinyl siding community.

These track-built Centex homes are now approaching fifteen years and the roofs are starting to reflect the age. Some of my neighbors got their roofs replaced and filed the claims on their homeowner's insurance due to hail damage and they only paid the wind and hail deductible of two percent which equates to about three thousand dollars. When I was married, we never had the extra three thousand dollars laying around to get ours repaired. Now I definitely do not have the extra funds as a single mom. The heating and air unit was repaired three years ago, and it is now functioning on its last breath.

Mom is waiting for me in the driveway when I pull up. My two thousand six Honda CR-V is so old and loud, and it shakes, but I don't have the extra money for that either, to take it to the auto shop to be repaired. I think it needs new spark plugs. Mom slowly eases in the front seat and says she wants to go the Page's Okra Grill today.

Page's Okra Grill is my favorite local breakfast spot, but it is just as good for lunch too. It's near the waterway on Arlie Boulevard. The restaurant is known for its home cooking, their Sunday brunch and their Bloody Mary's, which I don't drink, not a fan of tomato juice. 'They knew we were coming', as I always joke when I land a front parking spot.

It's crowded but we get a booth near the front hostess stand. I order the country fried steak and Mom orders a side of cheese grits.

'I need to start planning for what might happen after I am gone. I am worried about the jewelry because I know Jim would never part with it'. I think to myself it is her jewelry and what is Jim going to do with. Mom has already stopped wearing her jewelry as she really isn't dressing up in nice clothes anymore since so few clothes fit her shrinking body frame.

"Is there anything in the house you want? I want Marin to have my fur coat, since she lives in New York where it gets cold and because it will fit her". She is right that Marin needs the coat as it will never fit my five foot nine-inch large frame and it rarely gets below freezing in Wilmington anyway. Marin is shorter and smaller than me and it's a full-length brown fur that will look good on her with her autumn skin tone, and it will be perfect for when she and Rich attend those high society functions in the city. There is nothing I can think of that I want. Except I remember all I have ever wanted is the Bible that granddaddy brought back from the Holy Land forty some years ago that has a cover made from olive wood.

Mom does have a lot of jewelry, but acquiring her belongings is not something any of us are thinking about. Me and Marin and mom's sibling all seem to be taking it one day at a time in regards to her illness.

The waitress brings our meal and mine looks delicious and mom just doesn't seem to care that food is placed in front of her. Trying not to think about the fat nor the calories as I devour mine, mom stirs hers around with a spoon and takes about five bites and says she's done.
"Louanne will be gone this week for Thanksgiving, she's going to Winston-Salem, and she's leaving tomorrow for the whole week".

I ask her if she wants me to take off work early on Monday and Tuesday to come over to help her out around the house, and I tell her I will definitely come over on Wednesday since the office will be closed for the holiday. Mom says that she will be fine by herself. Louanne is the next-door neighbor that started coming over to the house every weekday precisely at three o'clock to help take care of mom, changing her bandages, checking the port, examining the wounds. She used to be a former Physician Assistant and she has several college degrees; one from Georgetown University, and she has an extensive medical background. Her husband Todd was married before and has adult children, but Louanne never had children. Mom and Jim aren't really that close to them, just neighborly, but mom's cancer seems to have given Louanne a new purpose in life. Louanne doesn't work and doesn't have a lot of friends and has no social life. She appears eager and happy to contribute to mom's recovery.

After I finish eating every bite on my plate, we decline the dessert offer from the waitress, and mom asks for the check. There's a consignment shop two miles away and I want to stop in to quickly look for a dress for Christmas Eve, in hopes to find something inexpensive. We pull in the Oakland shopping center and before we get out of the car, mom asks me to carry her pocketbook cause it's too heavy for her. We walk in the store, and mom immediately sits down in a club chair by the front door. I find a Karen Kane turquoise blue velvet dress to try on and then I walk out of the dressing room to the front of the store to show her. "Oh Scarlet, that is beautiful, it looks so good on you and the color really makes your blue eyes stand out. How much is it?"

"Thirty dollars".
"Ok, we are getting it" and she takes cash out of her wallet to pay for it.

We head back towards home, I drop her off in the driveway after telling her I will come over tomorrow to do their laundry, since Jim refuses to help out around the house.

■■■

The smell of the turkey is steamy and fresh as I pull it out of the oven after baking it all morning. Mom and Jim should arrive in about fifteen minutes. Jim expects dinner to be served at the exact time of the invite; unlike most people that will socialize before being served a meal. The stuffing is my grandmother Moore's recipe and I put it in the oven to reheat from cooking it yesterday. The green bean casserole and pineapple cheese casserole are both in the warming drawer. Last night I set the table with my fine white china and the sterling silver flatware mom gave me last month, the formal crystal water glasses and wine glasses. The silver set had been mom and dad's when they were married. Marin registered real silver when she got married so I guess that is why mom gave her silver to me.

They arrive and immediately sit down at the dinner table. It's just the three of us since my kids are at Stan's for the annual Thursday Holiday. I bring all the prepared dishes to the table and pour water in the glasses and open the bottle of Moscato Jim handed me. Mom and Jim both like that sweet wine. Mom says she doesn't want any wine. Although Dr. Jenkins told her she could drink alcohol, she doesn't seem to have a desire for it anymore.

Mom looks even thinner than she did yesterday when I was over at the house. Jim says the blessing and then afterwards immediately starts complaining about the church. He says the church is struggling financially as the membership is declining. I am thinking to myself 'aren't they dying off since most of them are old', but I keep my mouth shut. He claims some members have left to go CoastalLife Community Church, the sister spin off church that me and the kids attend located right across the highway. Then he says the Seaside Christian Church School is also struggling with declining student applications after the Vice Principal was found guilty of abusing dozens of young boys; a scandal that made national headlines. Pastor Rick and Libba spend a lot of social time with mom and Jim, and Libba is one of my dearest friends here. "He doesn't understand that his job is on thin ice with the decreasing offerings and some members are talking about getting rid of him." I try to change the subject to NFL football because the Carolina Panthers are playing later.

Mom and Jim leave after about an hour because mom is so tired and said she needs to lay down and rest. The good news is she hasn't been nauseous yet from this last round of chemo.
I clean up the dining table and the kitchen and pour myself a glass of Chardonnay and relax on the couch and watch the football game.

The turquoise dress does look nice on me, admitting to myself as I look in the newly renovated master bathroom mirror. Usually, I am modest about mediocre looks. I found some chandelier earrings on Amazon for twelve dollars that match perfectly that have turquoise stones with gold accents and hang about two inches long. My weight is down to one hundred eighty pounds, the lowest since Sheldon was born. Although I haven't been walking as much since I have been spending more time with mom after work, when the kids don't have a game or an event. The low carbohydrate diet must be helping me maintain the lower weight.

Mom had Josh remodel the master bathroom two weeks ago; completely gutted except for the tub. It's stunning with light gray tiled floors, black dual vanities with matching mirrors and chrome faucets, new Kohler toilet, and white subway tiled shower with frameless glass door and black and gray stone accent tiled along the knee wall around the tub. Mom doesn't tell me how much this project cost, but she claims most of her hidden cash is almost drained.

The house has been ready for the Christmas Eve party for three days now as I already decorated the table with the white tablecloths, and the center piece I made from an old mirror and placing white votive candles and red, white and green little stone pieces on it, and set out the small plates and my red monogramed on white cotton cocktail napkins.

People start arriving to our annual drop-in event. One of the first questions the kids asked me after Stan, and I told them about the separation was 'Can we still have our Christmas Eve party'? Both kids love this party, and they are now at the age where their friends come over to join the fun. Mom and Jim come after the seven o'clock church service. They always spend time during this party talking to Rich's parents, Richard and Lynnette from Delaware.

Later into the party, I take Marin and Rich upstairs to show them my new bathroom.

They both elaborate how nice it is and I tell them that I am embarrassed, "This was not a need, I could have continued to live with it being old, and I know I am going to need a new roof or new heating and air conditioning unit soon, so I would have rather mom saved her hidden money for that".

Marin says 'Well, mom isn't thinking rational right now with the cancer and the chemo brain and she's starting to get things confused."

'I know, but I wonder what she is telling Jim about me remodeling the house since he knows I have no money and I am flat broke".

Rich then says that mom is trying to prepare for when she is no longer here and she can no longer help me financially and she might be worried I may need to sell the house one day so just let her keep doing it.

We go back downstairs and enjoy the rest of the party. Everyone before midnight and I spend the next half hour cleaning up and loading the dishwasher.

I awake the kids around seven and we exchange gifts in the formal living room by the Christmas tree. As usual, not having money for extravagant gifts each year, I charged about four hundred dollars on credit cards to get them gift cards and a few items they each wanted. We then dress in decent lounging clothes to head over to Shell Island to exchange gifts with Marin,

Rich, and the boys. Dad and Darlene spent the night over there since they watch Larry and Bill during my party. The gift exchange takes about an hour since Dad and Darlene always shower us with too many presents. Then they leave to go back to Myrtle Beach, and Mom and Jim come over for another round of gift exchanges. Mom opens the gift from Marin, and it was a hand-made card with a trip voucher to Puerto Rico for the three of us. "I figured it was time for another girls trip", Marin says. Then reality hits, as all three of us are thinking the same thought; this will be the last Mother-Daughters trip we will ever take. This may also be the last Christmas with us all together.

Chapter Six: It's Back

I feel relaxed from the four nights of our vacation at the fancy Ritz Carlton in San Juan. It was my first time staying in a Ritz hotel. We had a great trip, sat by the pool located by the ocean each day, went shopping in Old San Juan, dined at several nice restaurants for dinner, and me and Marin had a facial in the spa at the resort. While lounging by the pool, we finished planning Jim's surprise eightieth birthday party next month, wrapping up the menu selection. Every day we had lunch in the Concierge Club, since Marin upgraded us to Club Level status. We also got free drinks from seven to seven and free appetizers from five to seven. I took full advantage and drank a glass of champagne with breakfast and lunch daily, not to mention again during the happy hour time. Mom handled the trip okay, she mentioned a few times she didn't feel well with having stomach pain and Dr. Jenkins has scheduled another CT scan later next week, but she was able to walk a few blocks at a time, and when she got too tire-some we would hail a cab.

The layover in Atlanta is about two hours long so we go sit at the food court area in the Delta terminal and I get Chick-Fil-A and mom says she is not hungry. "I am glad Marin didn't spend that much money, since I paid for the Italian dinner, and we got the free breakfast and lunch, so she only paid for two dinners".

'Mom, Marin paid for the Italian dinner' I correct her. "No, I paid for the Italian dinner', she says with certainty. 'No, mom, remember, the hotel gave Marin a two hundred dollars credit at the resort for the room check-in delay'. When we checked in, the concierge apologized that the room wasn't ready. They told us it would be a two-hour delay, but it ended up being four hours, so they gave Marin a resort credit. None of us cared about the delay because we got to hang out in the concierge club and eat and drink. We finally got to our room at five o'clock, in time to change clothes for dinner. The Italian dinner at Il Mulino had to be at least three hundred dollars because Marin ordered a bottle of Silver Oak Cabernet which was probably one hundred dollars. And she and I had main entrées, plus two appetizers the three of us shared. Mom ordered a side of truffle potatoes for her entrée.

Mom gets a puzzled look on her face as if she understands that she is getting confused and that her brain is not functioning like normal, thinking she paid for a meal that she in fact did not pay for.

■ ■

The parking garage is full, so I find street parking on Chalmers St. I'm a block away from the Harbor Island Club and my high two-inch heels are wobbling walking on the historic cobblestone street along the river. Inside the club, the receptionist leads me to the banquet room in the back of the first floor. I carry in the half dozen bright blue and neon green balloons to match the cake and invitation. I had the cake delivered earlier in the day and the cake was made to match the invitation, white icing with blue and green decorations. The guests should start arriving in the next thirty minutes. Jim is going to be surprised but he will be super surprised to see Darby Jones, his best friend of forty-five years from New Mexico, and really the only good friend he has. Jim's friends in Wilmington consist of a few church friends that are the spouse of mom's church friends, and a few neighbors.

Mom didn't let me invite Sharon and George and their girls because Jim had a falling out with her several weeks after mom's diagnosis and he disowned her and removed her from their Will. Mom says she doesn't know what happened, just that he was writing her off.

People start arriving, and aunt June and Uncle Wayne enter first, then mom's brother Daniel. Daniel also came to visit mom once in January and February and it appears that they are suddenly acting close, with him calling her once a week since after the Holidays. The church people are here and their next-door neighbors from the house on the left, Louanne and Todd, and Kim and Roger from the house next-door on the right. All in all, there are about forty people here including my two kids and Marin's family. They flew in from New York on Friday night for two nights.

Mom and Jim walk through the double glass frame doors and we all yell 'Surprise' from the back corner of the room as we are lined up against the back wall. Jim is stunned and acts appreciative and makes the rounds to greet everyone. The buffet food is good, and the open bar is a nice touch. The event lasts about two hours and Marin's family comes back to my house to stay because their Shell Island place is being rented.

We stay up talking until just past midnight; talking about mom being so sick, and how crazy her side of the family is. Their flights back to LaGuardia leave at nine-thirty in the morning. Rich has already arranged for a driver to pick them up at my house for the airport transportation.

They get back home safely on Sunday and I go over to Mom and Jim's for dinner later to socialize. Darby and his son were staying for three more days and Jim decided to cook out steaks on their back porch for dinner. I am looking forward to the week, and also for the next weekend to get here because I am going to Fayetteville for the weekend to see my high school best friends for a girl's weekend. It is a much-needed trip, as the stress of mom's illness seems to take a reckoning on me too. Ashley is hosting me and Peggy and the three of us have been best friends since junior high school. Peggy is coming from Cary which is about one hour from our hometown. There isn't a lot to do in the military town, but we usually have dinner at Chris's Steak house on Friday night, shop downtown on Saturday with lunch at Blue Moon Café, then an Italian dinner at Luigi's on Saturday night.

My cell phone rings Thursday just after three o'clock. "Scarlet, I am back in the hospital. I was having trouble breathing and I went to the emergency room and they ran some tests and admitted me. Dr. Jenkins hasn't been in yet, but he should be here after his office hours end". I tell her I am on my way to the hospital. I leave the office and head to the downtown hospital location.

This time she is on the fourth floor which is the cardiac wing. Jim says they haven't told her what is wrong yet, and then Dr. Jenkins walks in.

He asks mom how she is feeling with his usual polite bedside manner. "You have fluid build-up around your lungs. We need to insert a Pleurx drain that will drain the fluid' then he continues to explain the cancer has returned and how the cancer nodules produce fluid which is why her abdomen is swollen despite her being so thin, and that she needs to begin chemotherapy again in two weeks. The surgery to insert the drain will be tomorrow morning performed by a Cardio Thoracic surgeon. He also mentions that she is eligible for Hospice care but mom nor Jim make a comment and seem to ignore the word.

Mom and Jim both have a sad look on their faces, and I accept the news as I was expecting it, still believing it is the Lord's will to take her.

Dr. Jenkins leaves and mom and Jim don't say anything. I tell mom I'm cancelling my trip to Fayetteville.

She asks me not to cancel, that she will ask a friend to stay in the hospital with her at night.
But I know mom's days are numbered and I am determined to be by her side until the end. I will continue to be a devoted daughter until her dying day. I decide I will no longer make any more plans socially until after she passes because every-time I schedule something fun, mom has an incident and I go to her house for support, or to the doctor, or to the hospital.

The next three days are not fun; spending the night in the hospital each day, waiting to see how mom endures this surgery, calling and texting family and friends. It is exhausting dealing with a terminally ill parent. It is so emotionally exhausting it becomes physically exhausting. And I feel like I am neglecting time with my own children. Samantha's high school graduation day is six weeks away and I have yet to make any plans. She will be attending the University of North Carolina at Wilmington on an Academic Scholarship along with her Hope Fellow Scholarship that covers most everything except about fifteen hundred dollars each semester.

The Hope Fellow Scholarship is funded by the North Carolina Education Lottery and it is the highest scholarship awarded. It is difficult to obtain, especially at Hoggard High School, since the nationally known high school has over four thousand students, and many of them smart kids. If it weren't for the scholarship funds, I wouldn't have the money for her to go to college, and I am trying to figure out how we can come up with the extra fifteen hundred needed to pay full tuition amount due, but I have until the end of August to figure that out. It will be nice having her go to college locally, having her so close by.

It is difficult to get a good night's rest on the pullout chair in the hospital room. With the nurses coming in periodically throughout the night to check her blood pressure and vital signs, it is hard to sleep straight through without waking up several times. Mom is released on Sunday morning and I go straight home to shower and take a nap.

I am starting to worry about my job because I keep missing so much time off. I feel like my boss is getting frustrated with me. He is in his late thirties and never been married and doesn't have children, so he doesn't really understand family concepts. And now mom will start chemotherapy treatments again, three weeks apart, and I will need to take more time off to sit with her for those sessions.

....

Chapter 7: The Plot Begins

Daniel is now coming to Wilmington every other weekend and he stays at mom and Jim's house in one of the extra bedrooms. It's about a four-hour drive for him from Columbia, South Carolina. He decides to plan a mini-family reunion with June and Johnny's families; maybe since they all understand mom's time on earth is coming to an end, possibly by the end of the year. June and Wayne stay in their timeshare in Shell Island and their son Charles and his wife Stacey will join them. Daniel's youngest son Mike is married to his homosexual partner Brandon. They got married last year and Jim refused to go the extravagant wedding on Long Island, New York because he is certain homosexuals will burn in hell. Mike and Brandon reserve a hotel room in downtown along the riverfront at The Renaissance. Johnny and Sandy get a hotel room at The Hampton Inn near Mayfaire. We all plan to spend Saturday by the new pool in Shell Island. It's the first weekend in August and a typical hot and humid day. Johnny and Sandy, and June and Wayne complain it is too hot outside and they are too old to sit by a pool in the heat. Daniel is at the pool first and he secures two patio tables with umbrellas and four lounge chairs. Marin arrives next with the boys and Daniel starts conversing with her 'When you see your mom and she is crying, she is not crying because of the cancer, she is crying because of the Will'. Marin looks intrigued and asks what he means.

'Your mom is worried about the Will, because most of the money she and Jim have acquired is from her income, not his, and the Will has everything going to him first when she dies, and you and Scarlet won't get anything until Jim passes. She is worried he could change it, and it's mostly all her money. She knows how difficult he can be, and since he disowned his own daughter Sharon, she is worried what he might be capable of after her death'. Marin remarks that mom should do something about it since she is worried about it.

Mom and Jim arrive next and I am the last to show because I had to meet a sales representative from the Hampstead Heating & Air Company. My unit went out yesterday and cannot be repaired. Fortunately, there is a portable window unit in Samantha's room, so I slept in her room, and both kids spent the night out with friends.

While Jim was in the pool, I tell mom the estimate for the replacement unit is about sixty-four hundred dollars and I need someone to cosign for me for the payment plan since my credit is so bad. She says we will talk about it later when nobody is around, she doesn't want anyone to overhear us. We all continue to have a pleasant day sunbathing and chilling in the pool, and everyone is looking forward to family dinner tonight.

Samantha can't make it to the dinner tonight because she has to work. Sheldon had ball practice earlier in the day, but he showers and dresses in nice clothes for the dinner. On the way to the restaurant in the car he asks, 'who are all these people again'? I explain that June is mom's sister that he has met several times before, and he may have met Johnny once before and I am not sure he has ever met Daniel, and then I clarify that Charles belongs to June and Mike is Daniel's son, etc. Then I say, 'Grandma's family is not nearly as close as Granddaddy's family'. Sheldon responds, 'Nobody's family is as close as Granddaddy's family'. I quickly agree that is a true statement.

I have never told my kids about mom's brother Daniel and his big scandal. In the fall of nineteen ninety-one, I distinctly still

54

remember the day when my dad called me on my cell phone to tell me about Daniel's arrest. Back then the mobile phones were attached in the middle console of your car and I thought I was special having one given to me and installed as a perk in my job at USA TODAY. Dad asked where I was and told me to pull over to talk because he had important news. He informed me that Daniel had been arrested in Charlotte and the story has made the morning news. Dad saw the story and darted off to the Mecklenburg County courthouse to see if he could help Daniel make bail. Once dad arrived, Daniel had already been released. He had been arrested for soliciting sex from a male police officer that was posing as a male prostitute. Daniel was the Pastor of Palmetto Baptist Church in Columbia and was on a church business trip. Later that night the story was on local news channels across both North and South Carolina. In the morning the scandal was printed in most all major newspapers in the Tarheel state and the Palmetto state. I remember telling Aunt June 'I'm glad my last name is Moore'. It was astonishing to everyone because Daniel appeared as a macho man and he even played football one season for Georgia State University until he sustained a knee injury which forced him to quit. Nobody would have ever guessed he was a closet homosexual as he didn't fit the profile. I guess it shouldn't be unexpected that his son Mike is also a homosexual but at least Mike came out of the closet at an early age. I am not even sure that mom told Jim about that scandal.

The next week after the scandal broke, Daniel was fired from his job, and his wife Heather left him and filed for divorce. He has had difficulty financially ever since because he had trouble finding jobs. He was able to buy Heather out of the house in the divorce settlement.

Mike made the reservations at Elijah's Restaurant and reserved the Wine Room which means he has to guarantee our total bill will be at least seven hundred dollars. The Wine Room is located in the back of the restaurant and it's very private. Mom appears to be out of breath when she walks in the room, and I ask if she is ok, and she says she is not used to walking that far. 'What do you mean, didn't you valet park?' I ask. She replies 'no, Jim refuses to valet park, he worries that they may damage his car, so we parked behind the Subway'. I am thinking 'Seriously, he made her walk that far!!!'

It is a lovely dinner, and we all sit at one long table in the private stucco walled room. Mike picks up the tab for everyone and says it is an early seventieth birthday celebration for his dad and early fortieth birthday celebration for himself.

Marin calls me the next day on Sunday:

"Why is Daniel all of a sudden calling mom so frequently and coming to town so often"?

"I don't know, June keeps asking me the same thing. June said Jim told Mom that he never understood mom's family until Daniel started coming to visit. Not sure what that means. But June said it hurt her feelings because she and Wayne have been coming down every year to stay in their timeshare and they would usually have dinner with mom and Jim a couple times a year. Maybe because Daniel is single and has the time and he knows his sister is going to die. Mom did say it was nice to have him in her house because he waits on her, unlike Jim, since Jim still makes mom cook and clean as sick as she is", I reply.

> *Marin: "I have noticed how much more controlling Jim appears to be since mom got sick".*

Me: "Maybe he was always that controlling, and we just never noticed it as much until now".
Marin: "That could be true, and everything has always been "Don't tell Jim' with all her secrets from him as long as I can remember'.

Monday morning, I call mom to ask her again if she will cosign for me for the new heat and air unit. I am not sure how I can make the payment of two hundred twenty-eight dollars per month, but I have no choice at this point. 'No Scarlet, I can't do it, because of Jim, because he will find out since the paperwork has to come to my house'. I had already checked with the finance company and they confirmed if mom's name was on the loan, the paperwork would be sent to her address as well. Then my next option is to ask Marin. Marin becomes furious when I tell her mom refused to help me, 'mom is dying, she has plenty of money, she always says she was a bad mom, and this is a chance for her to be a good mom, this is a chance for her to do something for her daughter and her grandchildren, this a chance for her do something for her poor single daughter in need and she won't do it because of Jim! Give me the name and number of the company and I will do it'. I am not sure I have ever heard Marin so angry. Several hours later Jake from the company calls and tells me my sister paid for the entire unit on a credit card and he will install the new unit tomorrow. I am astonished that Marin paid for it in full, but she has that kind of money, she is extremely generous, and she is so disappointed with mom. I am not mad at mom, I feel perplexed. How can she be so afraid of Jim and why is she letting him control her so often?

This Saturday is Tax Free Weekend in North Carolina, the one time a year where people can buy school supplies without paying any sales tax. And it is always the second weekend in August, before our public schools start back. Mom had already told Samantha she would buy her a computer for college. It is recommended that the college students get a MAC, and Samantha has an old Dell laptop that Marin gave her for Christmas a few years ago. Samantha and I pick up mom at ten o'clock to venture to the Apple Store on College Road. We know the store will be busy today, so we want to go somewhat early to beat the crowds.

Samantha decides to get the MAC Pro which cost nine hundred ninety dollars, then mom tells the sales rep to purchase the warranty and she uses one of her credit cards to pay for it. Then Samantha asks mom if she wants to walk around the block to see her dorm room. The McAlister dorm is one block away as the Apple store is located in the heart of the college area. Mom says she is too tired, and that maybe she will go another time and see her room since she is moving in next Saturday. This way she will get to see it furnished and decorated.

We get back in the car to go back home when mom says 'Samantha, I want to pay the remaining balance of your tuition that is due.' I am thinking to myself 'whew, because the money is due in five days and I was planning to call Marin tomorrow to ask if I could borrow the amount needed. Mom continues 'drive me straight to the BB&T bank branch and I am going to take out cash to give you. Don't tell Jim I gave you the money. How much is due?'

Samantha knows the exact amount off the top of her head, and she says 'one thousand four hundred eighty dollars'. The bank is busy for a Saturday, and the bank closes at two o'clock and it is now just after noon. It seems like mom has been in the bank along time, like ten minutes, then she finally comes out with an envelope in her hand. She gets in the car and gives it to Samantha in the back seat. 'Here is fifteen hundred dollars.

Remember don't tell Jim. If after I die, he asks you or Scarlet about money missing, you don't tell Jim I gave this to you.' Samantha just says 'okay'. Mom is too tired to go eat lunch anywhere, so we go through the drive thru at Chick-fil-A. Then we drop mom off at her home.

June calls "What are you doing?" I tell her I am lying in bed watching Grace & Frankie on Netflix.

"Scarlet, I know all the stress is hard on you. You need to make sure you are taking care of yourself too. "I know, I am trying. I am just worried about my job because I keep missing so much time off for mom's appointments". I am really tired, and I don't feel like talking to her right now.

June asks "Have you figured out why Daniel keeps coming down? Don't you think it is odd that he and your mom are suddenly acting like they have always been close?".
"Yes, it is a little suspicious but at least it gives me a break when he comes, and mom likes it because he entertains Jim, and Daniel waits on her; cleaning up the dishes, bringing mom water, and stuff like that.'

June says, "Your mom told me she gives him gas money, and she paid for his car repairs last month".

Well, that doesn't surprise me, since mom knows Daniel doesn't have much money.

Chapter 8: September to Remember

Sitting at my desk on a Monday afternoon in the office, my phone bleeps with a text from

Louanne:

Do you know how many times I have told your mom about low residue diets? Do you think they understand that he was saying the cancer was back in her abdomen in February? Or that when he said hundreds of nodules on her intestines that those nodules are cancer? So glad you were with them today for that appointment.

My reply:

No, mom and Jim didn't understand the cancer nodules showed in February. When Dr. Jenkins left, she said 'oh, good, I thought he was going to tell me I had three months left'. She doesn't understand Dr. Jenkins doesn't really know how long she has left. Not sure either of them will ever fully understand until she's on Hospice.

I see my boss Jon walking down the hallway and I sense he is looking at me, like he sees me on my iPhone and he's thinking I shouldn't be on my phone while at work, or maybe I am just paranoid, but the truth is I haven't been able to focus on work and I have missed so many days and hours being by mom's side that my job is suffering. Several minutes later I get a calendar invite in Outlook from Jon for a meeting request for tomorrow morning.

Louanne emails again later in the evening after I have just finished dinner and sit down on the couch to watch 'Wheel of Fortune'. I check my emails on yahoo account on my phone.

September 7, 2015 7:14 PM Louanne Flager wrote: lfhoya85@gmail.com.

Scarlet,

I visited your mom today and got home a little after five o'clock. Both she and Jim said it wasn't good news and it wasn't bad news. I would not and will not tell them my thoughts, not my place. Your mom and I went over low residue diet, and she made a list – I even pulled it up on the computer for her. She made a list, and they are going to the store this evening to get what she needs plus her prescriptions. I know this is a confusing time for them. She mentioned she might have another year. I told her no one but God knows, and she agreed. Right before I left Georgia Sessoms came and brought them soup and cornbread which she can't eat. She did bring a big bowl of lemon Jello which Jenkins told her not to waste stomach space on. It's the thought that counts! She did eat half an egg salad sandwich while I was there, so she is trying. The problem is her getting full so quickly. Hope you are doing okay. I know none of this is EASY! The important thing is you need to take care of yourself too! Have a good evening.

September 7, 2015 9:03 PM Scarlet Gaines wrote: scarletgaines@yahool.com.

I will send you the recording from the doctor visit this morning. I am nervous about you being gone on vacation

61

since I can't keep taking so much time off work to stay with her every day. But maybe she and Jim will realize she needs Hospice soon. I called her Saturday morning and told her I was going to the new Nordstrom Rack to check it out. When I got to their house, I went inside because she wasn't ready, and it was taking her along time. I put the clothes in the dryer for her (Jim doesn't know how to use the washer/dryer). I had to drop her off at the front of the store and she just sat on a bench by the door. She saw the Church Secretary in the store and told her she can't do the Billy Graham calls anymore because it is too hard for her to talk. I told her she should get a Handicap sticker and she said she is eligible for one, but Jim won't let her get one. We then went to eat at Mosiac and she didn't eat anything. She took another nausea pill on the way home, and then said she hopes she has enough stamina to iron Jim's shirt. (Jim needs to iron his own shirts or take them to the cleaners). She said she was dreading tomorrow, she dreads each Sunday, because going to church is too tiring for her.

Jon's office is very spacious with a large desk and credenza, two big leather wingback chairs and a loveseat. I sit down in the chair directly in front of his desk. He seems like he is in a friendly mood, making small chit chat about him leaving for a hunting trip on Friday. Then the mood turns serious, and it his business-like voice, he tells me he is sorry that my mom is so sick, but I have missed a lot of work due to days off with her hospitalizations and doctor visits and my work performance has been subpar lately. He tells me I can consider taking Family Medical Leave Act. I simplify to him that mom probably isn't going to live much longer, and she will hopefully have Hospice soon, and I assure him that I will not need to take so much time off going forward. In my mind, I am thinking there is no way I could do that because Family Medical Leave Act is not paid and I cannot afford to go one week without a paycheck, much less a month or two. He reiterates that he is sorry my mom is so ill but he reminds me that I have maxed out my Paid Time Off and all leave going forward will be unpaid. 'Well, I don't have much of a choice, and it is doubtful my mom will still be here on earth at Christmas, I doubt she will live three more months'.

Saturday morning text from mom.

I am too tired to go to lunch today.

My reply: ok, that's fine, I will come over later to check on you.

Two hours later, mom calls and says she has changed her mind. I am almost finished getting dressed so I tell her I will pick her up in fifteen minutes.

Mom decides for today's lunch she wants to go the Apple Annie's restaurant in Lumina Station because she needs to pick up a prescription from King's Pharmacy. The Lumina Station area is very quaint with massive homes that were built hundreds of years ago and it is picturesque of what people think all homes in the old south should look like. The shopping district is no more than three blocks with the one restaurant, a bakery, a bed and breakfast, a few businesses and a few shops. King's Pharmacy is one from the past with a soda fountain counter offering milkshakes and fried bologna sandwiches. Mom needs to pick up a medication that has to be compounded and it's one of two pharmacies in town that has the capability to compound drugs. She says the medicine is to help with the sores in her mouth. The thrush in her mouth is a side effect from the chemo.

We go to the restaurant first for lunch. I get the blackened salmon salad and mom gets a side order of macaroni and cheese. She barely takes four bites and I eat everything on my plate. She tells me she is really tired today after she ironed Jim's shirts this morning. I beg her to stop the ironing and have Jim take his shirts to the cleaners. I have pleaded with her about this several times before.

My car is parked right in from of the restaurant and the pharmacy is not even one block away. We walk to the back of the pharmacy to pick of the prescription and she tells me she is too tired to walk back to the car so she stands out front until I can drive the car about fifty feet to pick her up. She is having such a difficult time with her breathing.

After I drop her back off at home, I go home, and I call Louanne and leave her a voice message about the day with mom. I never hear back from Louanne until Monday morning when she sends an email.

September 13, 2015 at 7:17 AM Louanne Flager wrote: lfhoya85@gmail.com.

Scarlet,
She told me Saturday afternoon that her shortness of breath is getting worse. She is okay sitting, but once she moves, she is breathless. She mentioned she got a blue jacket she might could wear in the casket. She is feeling bad all over. Jim is so far out of the loop it's not even funny, he can't even make coffee. Even when Jim is home, he may as well not be – she's still alone! He doesn't sit with her and talk; he is either taking a nap, working outside, working in his office, or running an errand. I am not saying this to sound ugly, it's just the

truth. I agree your mom needs some type of care. Karla will be coming over some which I am gone. P.s. Jim needs to take his own shirts to the cleaners!

June calls Monday night and I update her on the weekend.

'Scarlet, Jim definitely needs to take his shirts to the cleaners! How stupid! How dare he ask her to iron his shirts when she can hardly breathe. What a dumb ass! If I was there, I would tell him. I don't care if he gets mad at me. He can't hurt me, just hate me. Someone needs to show him how to use the washing machine, stove, and microwave. I can't stand the fact that she is dying and still waiting on the asshole. She needs to back off and tell him. And it makes me so mad that your mom wants to go to counseling to deal with her impending death, and Jim won't let her go because they can't find one that accepts Medicare for insurance. They have all the money in the world, and he won't let her spend seventy-five dollars for a counseling session! Ridiculous!'

My response:

'I agree that he is so unreasonable. I don't understand how or why she lets him tell her how she can spend her own money. And he got mad at me when I told him I told her friends to text her cause she can't talk on the phone. He said, 'don't tell them that, then none of them will ever call her again'. She said she prefers texting to talking. He is crazy!' We finish the conversation and I take a hot bath then get in bed watching television, waiting to fall asleep.

Email from Louanne Thursday morning:

September 16, 2015 at 6:33 AM Louanne Flager wrote:

I am leaving for our vacation tomorrow, so I went to your mom's last evening. She is trying to eat more, but still not enough. She is pleased that Karla and Kevin will come over some while I am gone. And she mentioned the Girdwood's were coming into town for a visit. Jim was not in a good mood. Your mom said it started with the pot roast she cooked that had too much fat in it for his taste. Then when she tried to eat the Starbuck's lemon pound cake, he insisted she was not allowed to eat it. She told him he was wrong, and he said he knew he was right. Then he went to take another nap. He'll get over it.

Karla and Kevin Proctor are mom's business partners. They co-list all their real estate listings and work together as a team and split commissions. They are empty nesters and in their late fifties. Kevin retired early from his executive career with FedEx and they moved here from Tennessee about five years ago. Karla always jokes that I am her sister from another mother. I am glad they are able to come over to visit with mom and help take care of her while Louanne is gone.

• •

Glenn and Gayle come to the house to visit with mom and bring in lunch in from Dog & Duck. The three of them sit at the kitchen table and catch up. Mom hasn't seen them if a few years. Jim is not around, and mom is not sure where he said he was going, but she said she thought she told Daniel and Jim the Girdwood's were coming by. Daniel is back in town again for a few days. He continues to frequent Wilmington more and more. Glenn and Gayle were my mom and dad's best friends when they were married, and they are were like a second set of parents to me. We used to spend a lot of time at their house during my youth; eating and playing games with their three kids and they had a pool in the backyard we would swim in. They still live in the same house today, forty plus years later.

They also still keep in touch with my dad, one of the few couple friends they had together that has continued to do so.

'Glenna, we are so sorry you are so sick. We love you so much'. Gayle says in her sweet southern voice. She still looks the same as she did forty years ago, short blonde hair and big brown eyes and her skin has few wrinkles.

Mom talks a lot as she is excited to see them, she tells them how she has to do everything for Jim; cook, clean, laundry, and how it is getting so hard for her since she has no energy and is so weak all the time. She talks about her Emergency Room visit last week, she was in so much stomach pain and couldn't breathe and needed oxygen, but Jim had her make scrambled eggs for him to eat before he would take her to the hospital. Glenn asks her why she continues to do everything for him, and she said she is too tired to try to challenge him. She goes on to tell them how she is so worried about what will happen after she passes, because Jim is so difficult to deal with, she is worried how he will treat her daughters. "I am especially worried about Scarlet, since she is the one that lives here." Mom tells them she is worried about the Will but that she is trusting that her brother Daniel will deal with any conflict that may arise. 'Daniel is going to have to handle it'.

A few minutes later Jim and Daniel walk through the garage door into the kitchen, Glenn says in his friendly upbeat voice 'Hey, well look who is here, how y'all doing? Where have y'all been?' Glenn always has been outgoing and humorous with a vibrant personality. Jim explains that he had a doctor appointment for his follow up from his carpal tunnel surgery. Daniel went with him for some unknown reason. It just appears Daniel likes to spend time with Jim. Glenn walks over and shakes hands with both Jim and Daniel, and Glenn makes the comment he can't remember in what decade he last saw Daniel.

Chapter 9:   Denial & Abuse

Jim's refusal to accept mom's illness is starting to wear on me and my aunt and uncles. Me, mom's siblings, and Louanne continue to communicate with each other daily in group texts and emails about mom's failing condition.

October 15, 2015 at 8:18 PM Scarlet Gaines wrote:

> Louanne,
> I will be able to go to the Dr. Jenkins appointment tomorrow because my business meeting was canceled.
>
> Mom and I went to lunch today and she said Jim was getting on her about staying in bed all the time. She said Jim was so upset about her asking if he wanted to go to New Mexico to visit, that she felt bad she mentioned it. She said it is hard on the caretaker. Then I said, 'Jim is not a caretaker, he does nothing.' He won't even go to the pharmacy to pick up the prescriptions. Jim doesn't wait on her. Then she said that is why she like for Daniel to come because he waits on her.

October 16, 2015 at 6:21 AM Louanne Flager wrote:

> Hi Scarlet, at today's appointment, your mom is going to ask about her diet so Jim can listen to his reply. I hope Jim will listen this time when Jenkins says she can only eat three or four ounces at a time! Your mom is tired of him bugging her and last week we finally decided when she drinks half of an Ensure, to pour the rest of it down to

drain. That way when she says 'it's gone' she is not lying. Of-course we all know that whatever Jenkins says today that Jim will not 'get it'.

I leave the office at ten thirty for the eleven o'clock appointment because I need to get gas and I am so hungry I want to go through the McDonald's drive thru to get a sausage McMuffin. I decide to save a dollar and not get a coffee, but their coffee is my favorite but the free coffee at the office will have to suffice today. A penny saved is a penny earned, I am that frame of mind. Mom and Jim's car is already in the parking lot and I walk in Dr. Jenkins office and they are already in a room. The receptionist behind the check-in window lets me in and tells me they are in room two.

Mom is sitting on the examination table and Jim is sitting in a chair. There is another chair for me to sit in. Mom decides to get up and go to the bathroom which is about five feet away. She is completely out of breath from trying to walk and she seems unstable. I ask if she needs my help and she says no. It takes her about three minutes before she comes out and walks back to the exam table. Dr. Jenkins comes in and I hit the record button on the phone like I always do to send to everyone after. He again stresses Hospice Care and how good of a program it is and talks about all the benefits. He makes it clear that medically there is no physical reason he can't give mom chemotherapy today, but he asks her if she feels up to it. He expounds that despite the disease being all over her body, her oxygen levels are at ninety-four and her CA 125's still at a normal level. Jim shouts 'between the chemotherapy and the Lord, she will get better'. Dr. Jenkins says that mom's time is limited, and that he is not sure she will be here for Thanksgiving. Jim lashes back sharply 'well, she doesn't eat enough, that is part of the problem'. Then Dr. Jenkins explains once again, 'As I have told you dozens of times before, this is a disease of malnutrition. The fluid in her abdomen makes her fill full and causes no appetite. That is why I keep telling you to eat French fries, milkshakes, potato chips, any high calorie junk food to get calories in your body'. As usual mom doesn't say much and let's Jim control the appointment. Dr. Jenkins says he will start prescribing oral morphine to help with her excruciating pain level. Lora opens the door and walks mom down to the chemo room. Jim leaves the doctor's office to go pick up a part he needs at Autozone, and I sit with mom for about ninety minutes until he gets back. I get back to my office and I am glad my boss is still out at a business lunch so he will not know how long I have been gone.

Later than night we get an Email from Louanne to me, Marin, June, Johnny, and Daniel.

October 16, 2015 at 9:03 PM Louanne Flager wrote:

Hi all. I spent a long time with Glenna after her appointment today. She is doing ok, but said it really hit her when Jenkins told her the disease was in her chest, abdomen and lungs. She also got fixated on when he told her he didn't think she would make it to Thanksgiving. Again, she was not really upset, and said she know she won't be cured unless God heals her completely. I cannot believe Jim dragged her to lunch afterwards, and to Lowe's. Glenna sat in the car while he was in the store. Him taking her all these places and making her do chores around the house is not helping her and making her illness worse.

I got her started on liquid Morphine. We only did .5cc and it gave her some relief with her breathing for about thirty minutes. She is going to take 1.0cc before dinner.

71

She can take it every hour. Hopefully, the morphine will give her some relief. Hope all is well with all of you!

They call themselves The Golden Girls: mom, Lindsey, Libba, and Maryann. They all go to lunch together every Wednesday and have been doing so for about two years. Lindsey is on her second marriage, as she was widowed in her mid-fifties when her husband died unexpectedly after having a heart attack while playing golf. She remarried quickly a few years later and there has always been something superficial about her, just not a real sincere person. Libba on the other hand is as sweet as can be and comes across as genuine southern lady. She fits the role of the pastor's wife perfectly, and she is slender and preppy. Maryann is in her mid-seventies; and she is a typical Southern Baptist who acts like she is better than everyone else because she goes to church and has lots of money. She doesn't have much personality, as she is quiet and reserved. She her husband Rory own multiple commercial real estate properties in the area. But I feel sorry for her because their toddler child drowned in the swimming pool in their back yard. He was their only son.

Today they go to Sewee Restaurant in town of Ogden. The small town and restaurant are located about fifteen miles from Seagate. The restaurant has been there a long time and they mostly have fried seafood, and home country cooking on the menu. Lindsey calls me after the lunch, after she dropped off mom at home. She says mom was down and depressed at lunch today, and doesn't feel good, and is so skinny and told them she has no energy. Lindsey says she is not good and is wasting away. Lindsey thought mom was getting things confused and was not steady on her feet when walking. Mom told them about what the doctor had said about her not being here for Thanksgiving. Mom said there is no sense in her buying new clothes because she won't have a chance to wear them. Lindsey says she ate a few bites. They asked her if Jim was still bugging her about eating and she said 'yes, he will until my dying day'.

As I am talking to Lindsey, I get a text message from Louanne that pops up:

got a text from your mom not to come visit her today. I think she's really depressed cause it is now sinking in she won't live much longer.

The next day, Louanne makes her usual three o'clock visit with mom. She emails me afterwards.

October 21, 2015 at 5:05 PM Louanne Flager wrote:

Just got back from seeing your mom. I can tell she has lost more weight by her face. Her eyes look sunken and her teeth look too big for her face. She is worried about her jewelry and how she can get it to you and Marin because she knows Jim won't give it up. She said June offered to get it out of the house for her. I told her when the time comes, I have a key and would go over when Jim is not home and bring it all to my house. She said that would be perfect and Jim would never know so that idea made her happy.

Mom's illness has definitely been good for Louanne, it gives her something to do. Helping my mom makes her feel useful and gives her something to do. She continues to email, call or text me after every daily visit. Today's email:

Just saw your mom, she is doing the same. But here's the funny thing. You know how you and I talked about Jim not understanding what 'family' is? While I was over there, she asked Jim if he wanted to play golf with Wayne on Saturday. Jim said, 'wait a minute, I scheduled us to play nine holes with Stan and Susan' and your mom said she couldn't play. Jim then said, 'you mean you can't leave June and Wayne for three hours?'. Then she told him she would tell Susan and she would understand. Then Jim finally let it go and said he would play with Wayne. I sometimes feel really sorry for your mom and some things she has to deal with concerning Jim.

On Saturday morning I text mom that I will bring her and Jim dinner tonight, that way she won't have to cook for him. I decide I will go to Foodies Café and pick up one of their 'grab and go' meals that I can bake. Knowing mom won't eat anything, I decide to get the chicken pot pie, because that is what I am in the mood for. I get to their house and Louanne is there and she is sitting on the couch. Mom comes out of the bedroom and sits in the chair they got from the Relax Your Back store. It was an expensive chair, like around two thousand dollars, but it is comfortable for her to sit in with her back pain. She has been in bed all day and she is complaining she needs to sit up for a while. After I put the pot pie in the oven I sit on the other end of the couch and talk with Louanne before she leaves. Mom just closes her eyes and seems rested during our entire conversation. Later that night I get this email from Louanne:

October 30, 2015 at 8:07 PM Louanne Flager wrote:

Hi Scarlet, so good to see you today and it was nice visiting at the same time, made for more conversation. I can tell your mom is changing her tune and she is thinking she is ready for Hospice.

Please excuse me in advance for what I am about to say – is Jim fucking nuts?!?! Those pills or elixir are not going to help her one bit and the high level of Milk Thistle may harm her condition. I don't mean to put it so bluntly because I know this is hard for you too. I know you understand reality, but Jim does not. Your mom is dying, and I don't think she has much longer left to live.

After reading Louanne's email, I send one to mom's siblings.

October 30, 2015 at 9:46 PM Scarlet Gaines wrote:

I got to Mom's at four o'clock today and she had been in bed all day. Louanne came earlier at three o'clock and Jim was asleep in his room until five. Mom said she is not going to prayer group tomorrow and not going to Bible study on Tuesday, but she will go to lunch on Wednesday with Lindsey, Libba and Maryann. She took Ativan this morning and morphine and she is losing her balance when trying to walk. Jim bought a bunch of cancer pills off the internet called PDQ Recovery that looks like a homemade label on the bottle, not FDA approved, and milk thistle and other herbs as ingredients. He also got PDQ Holy Water. He spent over five hundred dollars on the stuff. Mom said Jim is driving her crazy and that he told her he doesn't care what the doctor says, if she doesn't eat, she can't get better. She has not eaten today. My neighbor Patsy that was a Hospice nurse, thinks I should call Lora and tell her mom is ready for Hospice. My concern is she keeps going downhill so fast and can't function but will never get any help from Jim which is going to make it unsafe for mom.

Johnny replies back, 'if something happens to her, it will be on Jim's blood. Then June replies, 'the problem is your mom may want Hospice, but Jim won't let her have Hospice. He is such an asshole!'

I call Marin this morning on the way to work and she answers. She has just dropped off her boys at their nearby elementary school. 'Marin, I don't know what to do. Mom is going downhill so fast and I don't see how she can live much longer. She doesn't eat, she looks like she weighs ninety pounds, she is out of breath all the time, and she is getting everything confused. Her text messages don't make any sense.' I start crying.

Marin: "I know, the boys facetimed her yesterday and Bill made the comment that grandma looks scary".

Me: 'How can we get her to accept Hospice if Jim won't let her, if he won't let her stop chemo?'

Marin: "There is really not much we can do. Maybe you can call nurse Lora and talk with her and she what she suggests." That is what Patsy says too. I am thinking I will do that later, call Lora.

I get an afternoon text from Louanne:

I just got back from your mom's. She put a call into Lora and is waiting for her to call back. Her back still hurts and she sat with

76

the heating pad on the whole time. She has no energy and said she can't make herself do anything. She doesn't know if she can make the Figure Eight trip. She also talked about not going to church but the problem is Jim will want her to.

That's a relief for me; now I won't need to call Lora.

The next day I get another text from Louanne:

Have you heard from your mom today? I had a text from her that said she didn't want a visit today. You know she is going to kill herself accommodating Jim. He thinks her back hurts from sitting too much. His denial of her illness is practically abuse.
p.s. you mom has decided to go through her jewelry and split it up when Marin comes for the Figure Eight trip. She said it would be easy for Marin to take on the plane.

Me: 'No, I haven't heard from her. I texted her but she never texted back and when I called her it went to voice mail. Maybe she wants to be left alone today. Yes, I feel like Jim's denial that mom is dying is causing abuse'.

Chapter 10: A Time for Everything

On Saturday morning I go over to mom and Jim's and she is lying on the couch complaining of stomach pain and it needs to subside before we can leave for lunch. She says her breathing is getting worse and she thinks she needs an oxygen tank. I remind her that Dr Jenkins says once her oxygen level gets to ninety-three, she would need one, and she doesn't remember he said that. On the way to lunch she throws out the cancer pills out the car window. She wonders if she can walk the halls at the hotel at Figure Eight and questions if they have a wheelchair. She says she has gotten worse since she last saw Dr. Jenkins and she is definitely more tired. She wrote her obituary, and she hopes Daniel can stay for a few days after the funeral because she only wants me or Daniel to answer the door. But she says Daniel needs to work. She tells me she feels bad every day and her stomach aches all the time and she is constantly sleepy. She looks so skinny that her shoulder bones in the back are sticking up through her shirt.

Marin has planned a trip to Figure Eight for the three of us to get away. The five-star resort is situated in the northern part of New Hanover County and it is only thirty minutes away from Cape Fear hospital. She wants mom to get away from Jim for forty-eight hours where mom doesn't have to wait on him and can just lay in bed, rest, and look at the ocean. It is also my birthday weekend so we can celebrate that too.

On Thursday Jim calls me 'Scarlet, your mom is not doing well, you need to come over now'. It's after 2 o'clock and I know my manager is getting tired of me taking off to go spend time with mom. I send Jon an email telling him it is an emergency and I need to go be with my mom. The forty-five-minute drive back to Seagate feels like forever, because I am wondering if mom will die today. I storm through the front door and mom, Jim, Louanne are sitting at the kitchen table. Louanne and Jim are trying to calm mom down, she doesn't appear to know what is happening nor what day it is and she calls me June as soon as she sees me. Jim says 'we went to East Bay Deli after chemo yesterday, she ordered soup and she couldn't find her mouth with the spoon. She hasn't been right ever since.' What the hell is he doing dragging her out to lunch after Chemo? There he goes again; selfish bastard, doing what he wants, never thinking about mom. I immediately text Marin:

cancel the Figure Eight hotel NOW.

Marin's plane arrives early before five o'clock. Unfortunately, we hit the Friday afternoon traffic on the interstate after I pick her up at the airport. We make a quick stop at Verde to get salads to go for dinner. Since Marin is a vegetarian, she loves Verde.

As soon as we walk in the house, Marin hugs mom as mom tries to sit up on the couch. She tries to talk with Marin, but she can't seem to keep her eyes open for long. Jim comes home an hour later from his golf outing. He says he ate dinner at drank a beer at the 19th Hole. They both retire to their bedroom, and me and Marin open a bottle of red wine and chat while watching Property Brothers on HGTV. Marin says she cannot believe how bad off mom is. 'Why is mom not on Hospice'? I know mom is bad off, but It is different for me because I see mom every other day at a minimum, and Marin hasn't seen her since their summer vacation came to end the latter part of August.

I sleep in one guest bedroom and Marin is in the other. At five-thirty in the morning, I hear someone in the kitchen, I get up and go look and mom is making coffee. 'Mom, what are you doing?'. She replies, 'I have to make Jim's coffee'. Frustrated I say "mom, you are sick, Jim needs to make his own coffee'. She doesn't say anything and leaves to go back to her bedroom.

After Marin wakes up, I cook breakfast: egg omelets with sautéed mushrooms and onions. Jim leaves to go to Lowe's. Mom is still in bed and an hour later when she calls out to us 'Girls, come here please'. We walk in her bedroom and mom is lying in bed, and me and Marin sit in the accent chairs in front of the big window. Mom tells us to look in her underwear drawer and get out her jewelry. She has divided up the items into two Ziploc bags. The black pearls earrings are in my bag so I take them out and say 'mom, remember you always said these would go to Marin, to match the black pearl necklace she got on her honeymoon.' Marin and Rich honeymooned in the French Polynesian Islands and Rich bought her a beautiful necklace. Mom says that after she dies, the jewelry left in her jewelry box should be given to Samantha. We both thank mom for the jewelry as we each rummage through our bag looking to see what she has given us.

We don't want to drive too far to pick up dinner, so we order Wild Wings take out. Marin orders a salad, and me and Jim decide to get two dozen chicken wings, Red Dragon flavor. One of the few things Jim and I have in common.

At dinner, we are sitting around the kitchen table when Mom realizes she has urinated in her pants.

'Oops, I think I wet my pants'.

Me and Marin clean her up and help her put on pajamas. We then go to sit in the living room and Marin announces "Mom, I think it is time you start wearing Depends, adult diapers.' Then Jim then yells 'no, she will not wear those!'.

Marin and I just look at each other and don't say anything. Later, after he and mom go to bed, I say 'what is wrong with him that he won't let her wear Depends? He wants her to continue to pee and poop in her pants?'. Then Marin says 'I think that mom has battered wife syndrome, the scared look on her face when he yelled no.' It becomes clear that is why she has succumbed to his abuse during her illness; and why everything has always been 'don't tell Jim', everything always a secret, and now she has no energy, no clear mind, no way to continue to cover it up.

The next morning, while mom has gone back to bed after making Jim's coffee, Marin and I leave to go to the Wal-Mart. Marin wants to buy mom a water bottle with a straw to make it easier for her to drink to help her stay hydrated. She also buys Depends adult diapers. Marin says Jim doesn't need to know she bought them and that she is going to hide them in the house. They come in different colors now and look more like real underwear, so she thinks maybe Jim will never know, and hopefully he will never find out.

We go back to the house and Marin puts a few Depends in her underwear drawer and hides the extra ones under the sink cabinet in the guest bathroom we share. Mom wakes up and comes back to lay on the couch again.

It's now Sunday morning, my birthday, we need to leave mom's house soon so I can take Marin to the airport for her afternoon flight when I mention I look forward to going home for birthday cake because Samantha has made me one. Mom says 'oh, is today Sheldon's birthday?'. I reply, 'no mom, today is my birthday'. That is how confused and disoriented she has become. She doesn't even know it is her own daughter's birthday.

Text from Lindsey Lawton on Sunday night:

How did things go this weekend with Marin's visit?

Me: We waited on her all-day Saturday and she was getting used to it. She took morphine last night and stayed in bed until eight-thirty this morning but she thinks she didn't sleep. She has absolutely no energy and knows she won't be able to leave the house much longer if at all. She said she dreads taking a shower because she doesn't have enough energy to stand for a few minutes. Marin has decided she's got Battered Wife Syndrome.

Lindsey: That is not far from the truth.

Me: Jim didn't want her to have Depends but we got them and put them in her underwear drawer and got rid of the box. And we got colored ones that look like real underwear. She gave us her jewelry and said not to tell Jim.

Lindsey: I am so glad she gave you two the jewelry because she has been wanting to do that. You know as well as I do that she needs to use Depends. Jim is ridiculous. I hate that she has to hide things from him because of his absurdness. It is NOT about Jim. She cannot even be honest with him because she fears he will be upset. He is being selfish.

Me: Mom's family is starting to dislike him, and he is making them angry.

The good news is Dr Jenkins is mandating mom go see a Palliative Care doctor since she continues to refuse Hospice care, or as we should say, Jim refuses the Hospice care. I go with them to this appointment like I have been on every other; continuing to record the visit to email to Marin, June, Johnny, and Daniel. After the appointment and sending the recording, I email them all.

November 3, 2015 at 8:44 PM Scarlet Gaines wrote:

We met with Dr Richards today and a social worker was also in the room. The doctor explained Palliative Care. She explained that it focuses on quality of life, comfort, emotional well-being, symptoms and pain management. She explained the difference between Hospice care and clarified that you cannot have Hospice and still be receiving chemo treatment. So, she said she would continue to treat mom until mom agrees to stop chemo treatment or until Dr Jenkins says she is too sick for chemo. She explained to mom that it has to be a mutual agreement for her to stop treatment. If she agrees to stop treatment, then Hospice can come in that same day.

Mom told her that they don't know what is causing her shortness of breath (although the pulmonologist, thoracic surgeon, and Dr. Jenkins has tried to explain several times). Dr. Richards told her the cancer is causing her shortness of breath and drew a picture of the lungs and the pleural lining around the lungs and explained how the fluid builds up is causing the shortness of breath. Dr.

Richards prescribed morphine pills that will act longer, and mom can supplement with the oral morphine.

Finally, the doctor asked if she wants to die at home or in a hospice facility; if she had a living will, if she wanted to be on a ventilator, etc. She asked mom if she was worried about dying and mom said 'no, I have a lot of faith'. Dr Richards said mom should not be driving and should never have been while taking morphine.

The next day I get a text after dinner time from Louanne.

I had an honest talk with your mom today about Hospice. I cannot believe Jim is still refusing to let them come in. Both of them told me that last night when your mom was getting into bed, she slipped, and her head hit the headboard and said it was a hard hit. Jim checked for lumps and didn't find any but there is a red spot there. This is one more reason your mom needs help and needs a walker. She really needs Hospice soon. Also, she told me she had cleaned up her poop accident right before I came over; you could still smell it, she pooped on the kitchen floor. Jim is a hopeless cause.

I call June as soon I as read the text message and start crying. 'Mom is so bad off and it is so hard on me watching Jim treat her this way.' June tells me she can't imagine how hard this is for me and that she has no intentions to ever see Jim again after mom dies. She said she will call Daniel and Johnny tonight and the three of them are going to discuss how they can get mom the Hospice care she desperately needs.

Then the next morning I get a text message from Daniel on my phone while I am driving to work. When I stop at the stop light on Highway seventeen in front of the CVS, I type in my passcode to read it.

'Good Morning Scarlet. I'm coming down on Thursday night. Would you call Libba and ask her to have Pastor Rick give me a call at his convenience today or tomorrow? This weekend when I am there, I'm warning Rick that I am getting with Jim and just make him face up to the fact that Glenna is dying. I would like to talk to Rick before I come so we can have a plan to get this done. It is tragic to see someone love someone and do so much harm. Glenna is dying and we have got to make Jim realize it and that she needs Hospice care immediately.'

June calls me minutes later after I read the text and as soon as I answer, she says 'Daniel is coming down and having a talk with Jim. If Jim doesn't let Hospice come in, we three siblings are reporting him to the Department of Social Services for Elder Abuse.'

'Well, it's about time', I said firmly. We all realize that she may die from Jim's abuse before the cancer kills her. 'Daniel just texted me and asked me to call pastor Rick. And I can't go to the appointment tomorrow with Dr. Richards because I have a work appointment that I can't miss.'

I decide that I will send a text to the social worker to let her know what is going on.

'Hi Laurie, this is Scarlet Gaines, Glenna Reardon's daughter. My mom is even worse than she was on the last appointment with Dr. Richards. She continues to pee and poop in her pants and my stepfather will not let her wear Depends. She hallucinates throughout the day and doesn't even know my name anymore. She is falling down and hitting her head. I will not be at the appointment tomorrow. But if Dr. Richards cannot convince Jim to bring in Hospice care, then my mom's three siblings are planning to report him to DSS for Elder Abuse.'

Laurie calls me hours later and tells me she understands Jim's personality type, ex-Military and controlling. She says she will talk with Dr. Richards and she assures me they both will do everything to try to convince Jim mom needs the Hospice care.

Mom and Jim go alone to this appointment with Dr. Richards. Mom is hallucinating during the visit and Dr. Richards tells Jim that mom is going to die in the next few weeks and that she needs Hospice care right away. Reluctantly, finally he agrees.

Hospice arrives that afternoon after five o'clock and brings in supplies and equipment for mom's care. Mom sleeps through the night for the first time in seven months; thanks to the oxygen tank.

Libba calls on Sunday night and she says she went to visit mom this evening and she is concerned because mom is so weak and pale, and Jim said she slept most of the day. Mom told Libba she has to go to Novant Hospital tomorrow morning for blood work and Libba is worried mom can't handle the trip over there even with Jim dropping her off at the front door and Libba is wondering why Hospice can't do the blood work at the house. Libba offered bring mom a walker from the church and Jim declined. She says, "I have never met anyone like Jim".

I call Patsy to ask her why Hospice would allow mom to go out for bloodwork, and she doesn't understand why, so she tells me to call the Hospice nurse and ask, and tell her mom is too sick to go have blood drawn. Then I think maybe mom is too confused and really isn't having blood drawn. I drive over to their house and mom is asleep in the bed. Jim answers the door.

'Libba called and said mom is having bloodwork done tomorrow. Why?' I ask Jim.

Jim says 'I want to know what her CA125 levels are, so I can figure out what is going on.'

I say to myself 'What is going on is she is dying of cancer' wishing I could say that outloud.

I then ask if he will let mom use a walker to go tomorrow and he said 'no, she doesn't need a walker'. At this point I guess we need to all accept the fact the Jim will never be a caregiver. If she falls trying to get in the building, then he will have to deal with the outcome.

Louanne emails the next morning early.

November 15, 2015 at 6:06 AM Louanne Flager wrote:

> Just read Jim's Caringbridge update. You know what bothers me? Him telling everyone she has three months to live. If you recall that is what your mom said when they saw Dr. Richards the first time. Your mom said maybe I have three months left, however Dr. Richards never answered her. I know it doesn't matter, but I don't think it's right to tell people when none of us know how long she has, and it could realistically be much sooner than three weeks. Does it bug you too? I am sorry you have to deal with Jim's craziness. I plan on going over

around nine o'clock AM to visit and find out what is going on with the blood work. I thought about it on my walk this morning and Jenkins has in the past ordered blood work two weeks after chemo to check blood counts. Maybe that's what it is?

P.S. I saw Doug Hibben on my walk this morning and he had a lot to say! He said he doesn't know how to deal with Jim anymore and doesn't know what to say. He said when Jim starts talking about what your mom needs to be doing, Doug said his stomach is in knots. He said Jean wants to hit Jim.

I have a business trip to Charlotte and Columbia for work for open enrollment meetings for one of my larger accounts. Advanced Concrete has five offices in North Carolina, South Carolina and Georgia and I have to visit each location over the next few weeks. I go over to mom's house tonight since I am leaving in the morning and will be gone for a few days. She is sitting in the white recliner and I hug her and tell her I will be back on Thursday night. She tells me again she is sorry she was such a bad mom, and 'I love you'. She keeps apologizing at least once a month since her diagnosis, for being a bad mom. Marin and I try to comfort her each time we hear it, and tell her she wasn't that bad of a mom. Mom has always felt guilty for letting Marin go live with dad and Darlene. After I graduated from high school, mom moved from Fayetteville to Raleigh to start her Xerox career, and Marin decided not to move with mom, and made a decision to go live with dad instead.

I am sitting in a Japanese restaurant in Rock Hill, South Carolina because all the hotels in Charlotte were too expensive or booked, and the Econolodge is affordable and has rooms available. The restaurant is across the street from the hotel and I walk over. Jim calls my cell phone as I am about to take my first bite of the chicken tempura dish, 'Scarlet, your mom is not doing too good, I think you need to come home'. Really, I say to myself, nah, she hasn't been doing too good for months now and she has been dying for over a year. I reply 'ok, I have a seven-thirty AM meeting that will last two hours, and I will try to find someone else to do the afternoon meeting in Columbia for me'. I am sure my boss is going to be pissed when he learns I can't do one of the scheduled meetings.

After the ninety-minutes open enrollment meeting in the warehouse, to explain to the employees their employer is moving the health insurance plan from Blue Cross Blue Shield to Cigna, I drive straight through the three plus hours trip back to Wilmington, never stopping to eat despite not eating breakfast, and don't stop at all to use the restroom.

I arrive at mom's house before one o'clock and the hospice nurse is there and she tells me that mom is going to die today, she explains that mom is in active dying. She says she has stripped Jim of his duties, and that Jim is not allowed to go to the pharmacy to pick up more morphine, and for me to find the guns and get them out of the house. Lindsey and Libba spent the night in the spare bedrooms and they put mom in a Depends this morning and placed mom on the couch. They both had told the hospice nurse Shirley how Jim went around telling people that he is going to kill himself if mom dies. But we all know he was just wanting attention on himself.
I start texting mom's siblings and I call Marin to tell her to fly down right now, to immediately get on a plane. Daniel arrives about three o'clock and I tell him what the hospice nurse said and he promises me he will take care of finding the guns.

Mom continues to lie unconscious on the couch for hours, but they say that people in active dying can still hear you, even though they can't communicate. I kneel down beside her and say,

'It's time mom, you will no longer be in pain, you will now be an angel in heaven. You get to see granddaddy and grandmother and Tony. They are all waiting for you in our Father's mansion.'

Then Marin calls and I put my phone up to mom's ear so Marin can tell her goodbye. Her plane boards in a few minutes from the JFK Airport. She normally flies out of LaGuardia put she couldn't get a last-minute flight from there.

Mom finally passes away around five-thirty. The three men from Sturkin's funeral home come to the house to take her body within an hour after she has gone. Karla and Kevin bring over a prepared meal from the New York Butcher Shop.

June and Wayne don't make it down in time before mom died, so they check-in at the Hampton Inn and Suites before they come over to house. Marin orders an UBER to take mom's house after she lands in town.

We are all still sitting around eating the food and drinking iced tea. Then me and Marin go back to my house to wait for Aunt Paula to arrive. Paula is dad's youngest sister, and she drives from Alexandria, Virginia and gets to Seagate about ten o'clock. She loved my mom like a sister.

Me, Marin, Daniel and Jim will meet at the funeral home tomorrow morning to finalize all the arrangements.

Chapter 11: FAMILY DRAMA

Daniel and Jim are already in the meeting area with Funeral Director when me and Marin arrive. We all agree to select the brown wood casket, and we coordinate the upcoming funeral ceremony and burial. We feel the service plans are complete, and then Marin and I leave to go a nearby florist to get a floral spray for the casket. Then we go back to mom's house and pick out the outfit and jewelry for mom to wear in the casket, periwinkle blue blazer, crisp white collared shirt, faux pearl strand necklace and pearl earrings.

We start notifying everyone about the viewing on Friday night and the service at the church on Saturday morning. I copy and paste the details and send the same text to dozens of people, friends, family, and neighbors. I send to so many people and I really not sure how many and I hope I haven't left anyone out.

'Mom's viewing with be tomorrow night from six o'clock to eight o'clock at Sturkin Funeral Home on Bees Ferry Road in Seagate. The funeral will be on Saturday, eleven o'clock at Seaside Baptist Church on Clover Drive, with a graveside service to follow.

We arrive at the viewing at the Sturkin funeral home; me, Marin, Rich, and Sheldon. Marin decided to leave the boys in New York with Rich's parents.

There is an open casket and there are flower arrangements positioned around everywhere in the viewing room. The biggest flower arrangement positioned right beside the casket is one that matches the casket spray, and the card reads

'Thoughts, Prayers, and Love from the Julianne Moore family'. Julianne was my grandmother, my dad's mother, and all the siblings sent the gorgeous arrangement. There were flowers from neighbors of both mine and Marin's, and plants from my coworkers, and arrangements from mom's friends. People start coming in the parlor around six. There are so many people coming and going, I feel like I am at a wedding reception. Samantha shows up in a red dress and beige sweater because she came straight from campus and she got a ride from a friend. She didn't have time to go home first to get a black dress. I see my uncle Brett, dad's youngest brother in the distance, and Michael, my cousin. I didn't know they were coming. I am trying to make my way through the crowd to speak to everyone. It is almost seven thirty and everyone is starting to leave, and I see Brett, Paula, and Michael walking towards the exit door. I run after them and Paula turns around and I can see that she is crying. Brett says 'Scarlet, should we leave, should we not have come?' I asked what on earth are you talking about it. Then come to find out Aunt June has cussed out Aunt Paula and scolds her; 'your piece of shit brother Robby better not be at the funeral tomorrow'. And Uncle Daniel took Uncle Brett into the chapel and told him the same thing without the cuss words. I tell Paula, Brett, and Michael that it is ridiculous and that they all are welcome at the funeral and that mom would have expected them to come. She would appreciate their remembrance of her and supporting me and Marin.

Me, Marin, Rich, Samantha and Sheldon get in my car to go back to home. Marin calls Michael on his cell phone and he reveals to her more details about June and Daniel's behavior and she starts crying and continues to cry the whole way home. My parents have been divorced for thirty-six years, and mom has been remarried to Jim for twenty-six years. Mom, Jim, Dad and Darlene have been sitting together at my kids' ball games now for ten years. Why would dad not be at mom's funeral? Wouldn't he be there to support his two daughters? Marin is full of anger and shouts loudly 'Paula drove six hours in a car with a bad back to honor our mother and she gets treated this way'. Marin then announces she got an email from Daniel early in the morning saying June overheard me saying I had texted dad and all the Moore family the funeral details and how mom would not want our dad at her funeral. But Marin responded to him that our mom has been planning her funeral and death for seventeen months now and if she didn't want our dad present, she would have told one of her daughters that was her dying wish. Rich mentions he is getting suspicious about Daniel and says to Marin and me 'Is Daniel trying to get your mom's house'? We both are too discombobulated to think about something like that right now, and we ignore his question.

The next morning, we all drive to the church to arrive by ten-thirty before the service starts. We go to the conference room behind the choir room to meet all the family members and Pastor Rick. I walk out to go to the bathroom and run into Paula in the hallway and she tells me that as soon as she pulled in the church parking lot, June jumped in her car, opened the door and got in the passenger seat and started yelling at her again that 'Robby better not come in the church service'. Paula responded to her 'circumstances may have taken Glenna out of their lives through the divorce, but it never took her out of our hearts'.

I go back in the conference room and listen to Pastor Rick and the instructions for the seating. I am trying to keep my composure and trying not to lose it over June's rude and hateful behavior.
We go in the sanctuary and it is overflowing with so many people; some are sitting in the balcony. Out of the corner of my eye, I see dad and Darlene in the very back right-side of the

church along with Brett, Paula, Michael and my ex-husband Stan. I am thinking there must be five hundred people here.

Daniel gives the Eulogy and does a great job, talking about their Ledford childhood days, how poor they were, how they used to visit family relatives on a farm in Ridgeway, a very rural part of North Carolina, and how mom used to climb trees and broke her arm one time.

After the service, we are escorted by police cars to the gravesite, which is six miles from the church. There is a brief reading by Pastor Rick, then they lower the casket. There are only about eighty people at the graveside service. We all head back home afterwards; me and my kids and Marin and Rich go back to my house, while Jim and Daniel go to mom's house. Daniel is going to stay for three more days to keep Jim company.

The next morning, early Sunday morning, I drive Marin and Rich to the airport. They remind me they are coming back on Wednesday to spend Thanksgiving, since they already had the plane tickets because they thought it would be mom's last Thanksgiving and they were hoping she might still be alive when they booked the flights. Plus, it will be good for Jim for all of us family members to be around him for the holiday.

I skip church today because I am still too tired and exhausted from all the stress of the week. Later in the afternoon I go over to mom's house, and Jim and Daniel are sitting in the living room. I ask if I can see the guest book because there were so many people at the service, I want to see who signed it and who was there. Jim says he would let me read it some other time. Watching Daniel and Jim converse, I get a strange feeling, like they are treating me with a cold shoulder. They are ignoring my presence.

Something it's not right; Daniel just got close to mom once she got sick and he never came down to visit before she got cancer, and he never responded to any group emails or text messages, and I am convinced he is up to something. I don't feel welcome right now in my mom's own house, and I just get up and leave after a few minutes.

I wake up to an email Monday morning in my inbox, a group conversation from Daniel, June, Marin, with me and Johnny included.

• •

TO: marin69@aol.com; junelowden@gmail.com; jonathanl@yahoo.com; scarletgaines@yahoo.com
FROM: danielledford@sc.rr.org
RE: Flowers in church

Hi all,
Yesterday in church a Sunday School Class put flowers in church in Honor of Glenna and Jim. This was actually planned before this past week. You will notice one flower that was taken out of the arrangement and put in the spot where Jim and Glenna always sit on the second row. What a fitting tribute. Thought you might want to know that.

Jim is doing very good. Has his moments naturally but he is doing well. I will be here until Wednesday when I am going back to South Carolina for Thanksgiving. Glenna and I had talked about my staying some days. Jim has made plans to go to New Mexico for Christmas which is good.

95

December 20-January 4.
Daniel

On Nov 23, 2015 at 8:55 PM, Marin Oakley marin69@aol.com wrote:

Thanks for sending the pictures. It's very disappointing though to hear Jim will not be spending Christmas or any portion of it with us, the family he has had for the last 26 years. Mom made it clear, (long before 2015 when she had chemo brain, was hallucinating, and saying things that went against what she had always said prior to 2015), that she wanted us to continue to treat Jim as the family he has always been to us long before she got sick 17 months ago. The grandchildren, all 4, have known Jim as one of their Grandfathers since the day they were born. They have never heard of Casey, Jim's niece because she has never come to Wilmington since my wedding in 2001. It will be tough to explain to all of them, in addition to not spending Christmas, New Years, and Bill's birthday celebration with their Grandmother as they have since they day they were born, they will also not be spending it with their Grandpa Jim due to his choice to go to see Casey (whom they have never heard of) and his sister Jessica (who they have barely heard of) during their school break which is December 24 to Jan 3. Since Jim does not attend school or work, I cannot justify taking my boys out of school to come around his visit to Jessica and Casey. I do think it's good he is going to try and connect more with his sister and niece, but I'm disappointed he chose to do it at the exact time frame he has always spent with all of us for the last 26 years.

Knowing Jim, the way Scarlet, Rich, myself and all 4 grandkids do, we know he probably said things in anger and sadness over the last 17 months that did not present the full picture of his relationship with all of us to you all. He has been very close to all of us. I'm sure he said things like he thought we should quit our jobs to spend more time with Mom now that she is sick, kids should skip school or homework to spend more time, etc. As you know, people take out their anger and sadness on the people they are closest to. Not the people they see once every few years, or maybe once a year at most (Casey and Jessica). I'm sharing this with you all so you know that the picture he may have painted for you in the last 17 months is not accurate. We understand why he might do that just like we understand that him taking her out to home depot, restaurants, and other errands less than 48 hours before her passing was not done intentionally to speed up her passing despite the medical team telling us this would indeed speed up her passing. We know he did love and care for her despite how he behaved with her in the last 17 months.

Although mom fully expected (before 2015 when chemo brain settled in but when she knew her days were numbered) us all to spend Christmas together as we have for the last 26 years, we will support him trying to establish a closer relationship with his sister and niece in New Mexico. I just wanted to make sure you all know this is not what Mom would have wanted as she told us many, many times before her chemo brain arrived. Just as she told us many, many times what she did and did not want at her funeral which may have been different than what she started saying since April when cancer brain, chemo brain, and hallucinations where in full effect taking over her mind. We now fully understand the saying "of sound mind" and why you aren't supposed to make changes with Wills, funerals, or other things when you are no longer of sound mind. Mom had not been of fully sound mind since April of 2015.

There are other grandparents to spend time with to start new Christmas traditions. I promised Mom that would not happen, but I cannot force Jim to spend Christmas with his grandchildren. I just hope he is able to establish a closer relationship with Casey and Jessica so it will all be worth it.

I hope you don't mind me sharing all of that but felt it was important for you all to know there was a history of very close family relationships and traditions here, long before 17 months ago.
Take care, Marin

On Nov 23, 2015, at 11:39 AM, June Ledford <junelowden@gmail.com> wrote:

Marin,
I appreciate you sharing your feelings with us me).

However, Jim is 80 and with what little time he has left in my opinion needs to be about him. You are wonderful, what I have seen with your children and I know that you will be able to explain very lovingly with your children.

Jim is going to New Mexico over the Holidays with to be with his family. This year will be terrible for him. Personally, I never felt that you and Scarlet liked Jim that much even though he did a lot for y'all. I remember when

you sold your condo in Wilmington, he fixed up a lot of little things that needed fixing before you could sell it. Your mom did not ask him to he did it on his own. He has helped Scarlet fix up little things around her house. I know you feel like you promised your mom things and want to carry through. However, we promised your mom that your dad would not be at funeral and he was. It made me want to curse him out. All the grief and hurt he caused her and then how dare he show up. I don't see how he was there for y'all when you never connected doing the service. That is no longer my cross to bear but y'alls. I loved your mother very much though we were very different. She would want no hard feelings after her passing. She loved you both and her grandchildren so much. All of both of you were the love of her life and kept her going. Please know that Jim never said a word about y'all the last 17 months was difficult to watch her suffer, watching how he treated her, doing things she didn't feel like doing. But I truly believe Jim was in complete denial he and was not purposely trying to hurt her. We all are still hurting and saying things we will regret. I love you and Scarlet and our children love you as well. They still remember you coming to our house at Christmas when you were young. Again, I appreciate you sharing your feelings and we love you both very much.
June

On Nov 23, 2015, at 12:47 PM, Marin Oakley <marin69@aol.com> wrote:

You just further made my whole point that as outsiders to our immediate family you are not aware of our actual relationships and moms true wishes and I'm asking you keep that in mind when dealing with Jim. Jim and I have always been close. Your assumption that I did not like him could not be further from the truth. Please do not poison Jim's memories with false beliefs and false facts. The fixing up of one of my condos was not at all how you recall. It was because I care about him and was close to him is why I hired him and his friend to do some projects around my condo that were tough for me to do myself while living and working in New York. I could have hired a professional that would have done it in much less time, but Jim loved projects. With mom working and Jim not, having projects made him happy. That is why I chose the route that was more of a hassle for me, because I knew it would make Jim happy. That is just one example of how people who are not close to our family have no idea of the truth and should keep that in mind.

As for the funeral, I have not one doubt in my mind that there were no unwanted guests at that funeral. I don't want to speak for Scarlet but I'm pretty sure she knows this as well. We've had a close relationship with our mom for decades. She told us prior to being diagnosed that she thought she was dying of cancer. She told us at her 70th that might be her last birthday. She was very clear with us many times prior to her chemo brain and hallucinations how she felt about us and her funeral. Because of this, I have not given your thoughts about her funeral even a second of my time. I'm fully confident in what her wishes were regarding her daughters and her funeral. If she did not want our father present at the funeral, she would have told one of us during the 17 months she knew she was dying.

Marin

On Nov 23, 2015, at 2:51 PM, June Lowden <junelowden@gmail.com> wrote:

So sorry you feel the way you do. However, I know what I know to be factual.

We both loved Glenna in a different way. Don't forget we knew her for 72 years and felt every pain with her when your dad walked out for his present wife. It was not your mom's fault that they were divorced. I am so sorry that you never felt part of the Ledford family. We loved and love you and Scarlet because you are your mom's daughters, and she was our sister. I am so sorry you feel the way you do and my wish for you and Scarlet that you never feel the pains of life situation that your mom did.

I am not going to participate in any more he said she said statements. It will only lead to more pain.

We love you Marin and you too Scarlet,

June

On Nov 23, 2015, at 8:54 PM, Scarlet Gaines <scarletgaines@yahoo.com> wrote:

Dad was at mom's surgery, why would he not be at mom's funeral? The two of them had been communicating during her illness, via her new private email address. If mom didn't want dad at the funeral, she would have told him, she would have told me, she would have told Marin. And Marin and I gave Jim an 80th birthday party where Marin and Rich paid about $5000 for the party at the Harbor Island Club (I only bought the cake, balloons and invitations). Jim's party was nicer and more costly than the 70th birthday party we gave mom. And you people think we don't like him? We didn't like

how he treated her during her illness, and we don't like you or Daniel influencing him now about how he should spend his Christmas holiday.
Scarlet

On November 23, 2015, at 9:03 PM, June Lowden junelowden@gmail.com wrote:

Please stop this immature crap. Bottom line is we differ. Your dad is your dad and you love him which is understandable. He is not my father and I have no respect for him or the way he did you all or my sister. Now go to bed and stop this crap. Do not send me another email regarding this; now grow up and go to bed.
June

I call Lindsey Lawton and tell her about the family drama; 'Scarlet, that is silly, your mother would expect your father to be at the funeral. In the fifteen years that we have been friends, I never heard her speak badly of your dad. She always said she was a bad mom, and that she is thankful you and Marin are so close to your dad and his side of the family.'

Chapter 12: Disownment

Marin and Rich and the boys arrive Wednesday night before Thanksgiving and once again their Shell Island place is rented so they are staying with me. With Samantha living in the dorms and her dorm the only one open during the Holidays, Rich and Marin stay in her bedroom and the boys stay in the guest bedroom. Marin says, 'Jim called me last night and asked if me and Rich only would come meet with him tomorrow morning at his house at ten o'clock and leave the boys with you.'

Me: 'What, that is weird, what for? I texted him this morning asking him if we can eat at noon tomorrow, but I haven't heard back from him'.

Marin: "I don't know, but I am petrified. I cannot imagine anything except he is mad that our dad came to the funeral.'

I had worked all day earlier getting the dining table set with my fine china, and the real silver flatware. I premade some of the side dishes to bake tomorrow and thawed the turkey in the refrigerator.

Marin, Rich and I open a bottle of red wine, and stay up past midnight talking about the drama with June.

Marin says, 'I cannot believe mom left us nothing'. I said 'Yep, nothing.' All she left us was a manila folder for each one of us that she gave Louanne to give us. Louanne had dropped them off at my house Monday morning. In mine was an old picture of granddaddy and grandma, a picture of me, my dad, and mom when I was about three years old, a Mother's Day card I gave her when I was five, and my college graduation announcement.

Marin's folder has granddaddy's obituary, a picture of the four of us when she was four and I was nine, and a letter to Judy. Marin asks, 'who is Judy'? I respond, 'I don't know, what are you talking about?'. She says 'look at this letter:

Dear Judy,
Here are my ambitions and the goals I have for my life; a sailboat in Virgin Gorda, a red Porsche 911, a house with a glass sunroom with a jacuzzi, wearing designer clothes until I am eighty years old, shopping trips to New York City every year to buy the designer clothes, and to make a six-figure income each year until I retire at age seventy.

Marin then says, 'these are all things our dad would never want'. Then I reply 'maybe our dad got tired of the financial pressure of trying to keep mom happy with material things, and he was looking for a way out of the marriage. After they separated, Grandmother Moore told me that first Christmas that mom always said she was going to drive a nice car and live in a big house.' Marin says she remembers that first Christmas without dad because she remembers all the Moore family coming over to our dumpy apartment and showering us with gifts, and the Ledford family never came around to visit. And I remember from my earlier childhood days, the time that dad took me to The Capitol, an upscale local department store on Hay Street one Christmas Eve to buy mom that fur coat as her present. I think I was in fifth grade then. I remember the townhome at Sunset Beach and the Jeep in the driveway; an extra vehicle specifically used for the beach trips on weekends. It does make sense now, that dad didn't want all those material possessions, and it could have been difficult for him to try to keep up the lifestyle mom wanted or maybe she demanded.

Marin starts worrying about the meeting Jim in the morning, and says she is panicking and scared to death because she cannot imagine what it is about. Why would Jim be mad if Dad came to the funeral? The four of them have been getting along with years. Our minds start to wonder and then we start thinking that maybe dad had an affair with someone else before Darlene. Maybe that is why June and Daniel hate our dad so much. June always says, 'you girls don't know everything'.

Marin and Rich leave the house at nine fifty-five since mom and Jim's house is three fourths of a mile away in the same development, they will arrive on time. I continue cooking and Samantha and Sheldon try to entertain Larry and Bill with video games, television, and playing in the garage. I have everything ready for our first Thanksgiving dinner without mom. Reality is, it's only been six days since she passed away and it hasn't really sunk in yet that she is gone, even though I've been trying to prepare mentally for seventeen months. But the drama with June and Daniel has made it more difficult to grasp.

It is now almost one o'clock and Marin and Rich are not back. We were supposed to eat at noon and all the food is ready in the oven and the warming drawer. I sit on the front porch bench waiting, and finally, I see their rental car turn the corner, and move down the street into my driveway. They both get out and walk to the front porch 'Jim's not coming'. I am baffled as to what is going on. Then they both start to talk, going back and forth, bouncing off each other. They sat at mom's kitchen table and Jim pulled out a piece of paper and said he would no longer have a relationship with me or my kids and listed these reasons why written down on the paper. Marin starts repeating Jim's words:

'You didn't come over every day when mom was sick'.

'You ate M&M's out of the bowl on their kitchen counter the day she died'.

'He didn't like the food you brought over one day from Baja Tower'.

I am starting to shake because I am not believing this. I have a stunned look on my face.

'He didn't like the red dress Samantha wore to the viewing'.

'Samantha didn't come over enough when mom was dying'.

'Sheldon doesn't do enough yard work'.

Then she stops and says she cannot think of everything he said.

Then Rich chimes in again, 'The Honda Accord would have lasted longer if Sheldon had taken better care of it. He doesn't like it that Sheldon drives Samantha's car.'

'He didn't want my dad at the funeral, but he saw his name and Darlene's in the guest book and now knows he was there.'

'I don't have any money, yet I was able to fix up my house.'

Then Marin explains she said to Jim, 'Well, mom had some secrets. Scarlet truly doesn't have any money and mom used her own money to fix up Scarlet's house. Mom planned the home projects with her contractor, it was someone mom knew, and she had used him to fix up the houses she had listed for sale. Mom paid the contractor directly to do all the work to fix up her house." Marin said Jim looked dumbfounded. Jim also said to them that he was not going to give Samantha the jewelry that mom left for her in the Will. And he said he was mad that mom gave me and Marin the jewelry and he was mad that mom secretly met with an attorney to leave us the jewelry in her Will.

Mom had met with the attorney on the military base the week we got back from Puerto Rico. She must have understood she was losing her mind and wanted to get it itemized before she passed. Jim told Marin and Rich that Daniel is the only person in the family he trusts now. Marin finally told him they needed to leave to go have dinner as me and my kids and her kids are waiting for Thanksgiving Day Dinner.

I really didn't know what to say or think. The three of us still standing on the front porch. 'What are we all going to tell the kids?' There is a place setting at the table for Jim and now it going to be left empty. We go inside the house and Marin tells the kids, 'Jim is not coming to dinner today. He is still too sad from grandma dying to come over'. None of the kids make a comment and we all sit down to eat. Rich says grace and I can't seem to hear or think right now. I have definitely lost my appetite.

I somehow muddle through the dinner and we all make plans to go 'gray Thursday shopping' since it is the night before Black Friday. All seven of us go and stand in the long line waiting for Target to open; we wait at least forty-five minutes before we make it inside the store to take advantage of the good deals. While in Target, dad calls my cell phone; Marin must have already called and told him everything; and I just break down crying in the middle of the store. I am balling so hard I cannot stop, and I have to leave to go walk outside. 'I was by my mother's side for seventeen months; I was at every doctor's appointment except maybe one or two, I was at every hospitalization and surgery and spent numerous nights with her,

Chapter 12: The Email

It's Sunday morning I am still tired from everything, I drink my morning coffee while reading the Wilmington Star Newspaper. Then I go to my computer to check Facebook and then my emails. In my inbox is the weekly devotional from Doug Hibben down the street. He added me to the church Sunday School class email list a few months ago as everyone on the list was communicating with me about mom's illness.

Date: Sun, 29 Nov 2015 7:34 AM Doug Hibben
<douglashibben37@gmail.com>

Subject: Re: A Good Sunday Morning Lesson and
Message.........."When Opposition Strikes"

One can always identify a "true" fan. Everything he or she is wearing and carrying displays the team and school colors and/or its logo.

And I'm no exception. Ready to scream and cheer my team onto victory......
Go TARHEELS! This confidence and bravado can feel very different however
at an away game, especially if you find yourself surrounded by fans of the opposing team. You find yourself now in somewhat "hostile" territory. You may even feel threatened at times as you cheer for your favorite team.

Opposition is a part of life. It makes for a great football or basketball game, tennis match or the Kentucky Derby and the "Run For The Roses" that first Saturday in May. But in most other areas of life, we typically don't welcome opposition.

In an infinitely greater way, this is reality for all those who choose to follow Christ.
Living for Christ in a hostile, "worldly" culture is not easy. Opposition to Christ and
His followers is certainly nothing new. Those opposed to Christ and His followers may believe we are on the wrong side of history, but we're NOT on the wrong side of truth.

So how do we respond? The early church responded to opposition in prayer. Maybe it's time we do the same.

And the Lord responded to their believing prayer and empowered the church to advance the gospel in the midst of persecution.

We can boldly face any opposition because God is in charge

It's now been three days since Jim disowned me and I decide to reply to him and the other Sunday School Class members to ask for prayers and inform them about Jim disowning me and my children and how he treated my mother.

On November 29, 2015 8:13 AM Scarlet Gaines <scarletgaines@yahoo.com>

Subject: Re: A Good Sunday Morning Lesson and

Doug, yes, please do pray for Jim Reardon as he is NOT the man of God he proclaims to be and the two of us are definitely on opposing sides.

I watched my mother die for seventeen months of peritoneal cancer. I was by her side for five hospitalizations, one outpatient procedure, twelve chemo treatments, Emergency Room visits, and numerous doctor's appointments. I spent many nights in the hospital with her and countless hours with her at home as well as being present for most every doctor's appointments. I spent every Saturday with her as I did not know how many Saturdays she would have left. I have had no life for myself for seventeen months as my devotion was to my mother (canceled trips, parties, social events, etc.).

I also had to watch Jim abuse my mother for months. After every Chemo or hospitalization or doctor's appointment, he would drag her to Home Depot or Lowe's or lunch. The Saturday she was released from major surgery (she had several sections of colon and small intestine removed and one hundred tumors), he dragged her to Lowe's and Ace Hardware on the way home. He would drag her to Home Depot after each Chemo treatment where she would have to walk to the back of the store to use the bathroom. On November 5 after Chemo, she could barely walk to the car after, yet he dragged her to East Bay Deli where she almost fell asleep at the table and could not find her mouth with her spoon. Up until her dying day he had her make his coffee at five AM, do his laundry, and cook his dinner. She was not stable and falling down yet he refused to let her use the walker. She fell once and hit her head by her bed. She was confused and hallucinating and peeing and pooping in her pants. He refused to let her wear Depends leaving my mom or her friends to clean her up. He forced her to go the Church many times and she blatantly told him she did not want to go to the Sunday School party in Onslow because she didn't feel up to, but he told her she had to go because she RSVP'd. And when she told Jim she didn't want to go to prayer group because she was too tired and felt too bad, he told her she could get dropped off at the door, then walk in and rest on the bench for a few minutes, then walk to the room and just sit there for two hours. He refused to let Hospice come in when Dr. Jenkins first mentioned Hospice in July. Hospice was mentioned at every doctor's appointment thereafter and not only by Dr. Jenkins but by all the other doctors. The night before the last appointment with Palliative Care Dr. Richards, I texted that Social Worker, that mom was hallucinating, confused, no longer of sound mind, peeing and pooping in her pants and Jim refusing Depends, falling down and hitting her head, and that if Jim did not agree to let Hospice come in, my mom's siblings were calling Department of Social Services to report Jim for Elder Abuse. Fortunately, Dr. Richards did a great job handling Jim and Hospice came in that night, and mom was put on other medications and Oxygen and she slept through the night for the first time in months. However, Jim still continued to abuse her, still made her wait on him and make his coffee and cook his dinner and refused to let her use the walker and still refused to let her wear Depends. On Monday, November 16, two days before mom passed, Jim dragged her to Novant Hospital for bloodwork (no longer required because she was now under Hospice care and not Dr. Jenkins) because Jim wanted to know what her CA125 levels were (even though the doctor said at every appointment that mom's CA 125 levels always showed inaccuracy). He then dragged her to the doctor's office for a B12 shot. My sister then called the Hospice nurse to tell her and the Nurse was horrified and instructed Jim to not let mom leave the house. On Wednesday, the Hospice Nurse told me she

112

stripped Jim from any responsibility for caring for mom and put Lindsey, Libba, and Louanne in charge of mom's care in the home. Mom only had Hospice care for seven days due to Jim's negligence and abuse. She was eligible for Hospice in July.

Now Jim is blaming me for everything, the daughter who gave up her life to be with her mother for seventeen months. Jim called a meeting with my sister and brother-in-law hours before our scheduled Thanksgiving Day dinner. He told him he would no longer have a relationship with me or my children because of the following reasons:

1. He did not like the food I brought over from Baja Tower about ten days before her death.

2. He doesn't understand how I can have a relationship with my father after what he did to my mom (my parents have been divorced for 38 years and my sister also has a relationship with my dad).

3. I ate M&M's out of the bowl while my mom was dying and was texting (I had an early meeting in Charlotte that morning and then drove straight to mom's house and had no breakfast or lunch nor any food and I was texting my sister about my mom, telling her she needed to get on the next plane to Wilmington).

4. Jim doesn't like my mom's sister June and he doesn't understand why I talk to her or have a relationship with her.

5. I stroked my daughter's hair one day at their house, but didn't I stroke my mother's hair.

6. My daughter only came to see mom five times since she went to college in August. She didn't come over enough this summer (even though she had a full-time job and worked about 40 hours a week or more)

7. He hasn't seen my son in three months (which is a flat out lie, as my son was at the house probably four times since school started).

8. My son doesn't do enough yard work (he mows the grass every other week if he is home as he plays Hoggard Varsity basketball and travel basketball, but he is injured now on crutches, and had an injury this summer, was on crutches, so he was not physically able to mow the grass).

9. It bothers him that my son drives my daughter's car (my daughter is not allowed a car as a freshman in college so why would I let the car just sit in the driveway when my son can use it for school and practice)?

10. The 2000 Honda Accord that had one hundred eighty thousand miles on it would have lasted longer if my son had taken better care of it. (I didn't have the eighteen hundred dollars to have it repaired when it died).

11. Mom's next-door neighbor Louanne came over every day to visit with mom, yet I didn't come

over every day (I have a full-time job and I missed countless days and hours of work to be with my mom during her illness).

12. Jim didn't like the red dress my daughter wore to viewing (she came straight from Friday afternoon class and didn't have many dresses in her college closet, but she knew she would have a black one at home for the funeral).

Jim is nothing but heartless and a hypocrite. He needs prayer.

My mom secretly went to their attorney in March and itemized the distribution of her jewelry. She gave these items to me and my sister on November seventh, but the Will states all remaining jewelry is to be given to my daughter Samantha. Jim told Marin and Rich that he will not give Samantha the jewelry.

When my Heating and Air unit went out this summer, I needed someone to cosign to get zero interest for monthly payments for three years for a new unit. Mom couldn't cosign because Jim wouldn't let her. What kind of Christian parent wouldn't do something so simple to help a struggling single mom in need?

Jim has complained repeatedly all year because he found a receipt for the eighty-nine dollars mom spent on my nephew's Christmas present and he thought that was too much money for my mom to spend on a grandchild.

We also believe my mom's brother Daniel Ledford is trying to have me written out of the Will and have me replaced with himself. Daniel was arrested decades ago for soliciting a male prostitute; then lost his job and his wife. So, he has struggled financially ever since.

How can Jim be like this and proclaim to be a man of God? He thinks he is such a great Christian. Yet, he disinherited his own blood daughter and grandchildren in California who are non-Believers. Now he is disowning me and my children.
Pray for me that I can find some way to forgive what he has done to my mom, and now me and my children.
Scarlet

Chapter 13: The Lawsuit

Me to Marin:

Don't you think I should let Sharon know mom has passed.

Marin: yes, you should call her or email her.

I decide I will email her now because I don't have her phone number.

December 1, 2105 at 10:10 PM Scarlet Gaines wrote: scarletgaines@yahoo.com

> Sharon,
> Hope you and George and the girls are doing well. I just wanted to let you know that mom passed away on November 18. And I wanted you to know that your dad has disowned me and my children.
>
> Jim is blaming me for mom's death and refused to come over to Thanksgiving dinner. He had a three-hour meeting with Marin and Rich before our scheduled Thanksgiving Dinner. Jim doesn't understand how I can have a relationship with my dad after what he did to my mom, I ate M&M's when came over when mom was sick, I stroked Samantha's hair over at moms but didn't stroke mom's hair, Jim didn't like the dress Samantha wore to funeral, it bothers him that I let Sheldon drive Samantha's car, Sheldon doesn't do enough yard work, Louanne (next door neighbor) came over every day at three o'clock but I didn't come over every day, Samantha had only been to

their house five times since she went to college and didn't come over enough this summer when she was working, Sheldon doesn't come over enough, the 2000 Honda that had one hundred eighty thousand miles would have lasted longer if Sheldon took better care of it, he didn't like the food I brought over from Baja Tower, etc.

I can only imagine how you feel about him. I am trying really hard to not hate him but it is very difficult. Jim has been my kid's grandpa since they were born, and I had to tell them he doesn't want to be their grandpa anymore. I can totally understand how difficult it must be for you to have a father that isn't a father. The sad thing is Jim proclaims to be a Christian yet there is nothing about his actions that are Christian. I always felt he has a responsibility as a father and a Christian to set an example for you and he clearly has not done that. The Bible says we are to love and forgive everyone, but I don't think Jim is ever sorry for his unloving behavior. I don't think Jim knows how to love anyone. My mother is the only person that ever loved him, and he treated her like a possession, not a person, which is not true love. It's almost as if she became a battered wife, and he controlled her until the very end, refusing to let her get Hospice, not letting her wear Depends despite her peeing and pooping in her pants, refusing to let her use a Walker, making her wait on him until her dying day; making his coffee, cooking his meals, forcing her to go to parties and church, etc.

I am so sorry he has been such a bad father to you, so sorry he doesn't set a Christian example like he should, sorry that his disowned you too, which against the Lord's word.

Love, Scarlet

December 2, 2015 at 2:12 PM Sharon Garner wrote:
sgcaligirl@gmail.com

Hi Scarlett,
I was wondering how he wasn't showing through what kind of person he really was. He only went to church to meet a woman. He was never a Christian before. My childhood was full of emotional and physical abuse. My mom left when I was fourteen to live with his mother from her urging to get away from him. I left home at seventeen as soon as I graduated and never wanted to see him again. He was brutal to Tony, suffered many beatings. Tony was already alcoholic in junior high, using heroin in ninth grade, he was sent away to live with grandmother who then died of heart attack. Tony was constantly seeking approval, never learned that he wasn't the bad one. He was told over and over again and he was worthless and would never amount to anything. At the Tony's funeral my dad was so mad that Tony left everything to my mom and nothing to him. Your mom kept telling me how I had to forgive him and then my dad called and started yelling at me and it brought up my childhood all over again. I had horrible flashbacks and saw a therapist, she agreed would be best to end relationship. Further conversations with him got very nasty, he would bring up all kinds of things, Leslie doesn't call him enough, George didn't offer him a chair, etc. I finally said why don't we end this right now and he said fine, and that was it. I really feel so relieved that I don't have to see him anymore. Glenna never knew anything, and I knew she was upset with me and that was the hardest part. She was such a sweet lady. I never could understand how she ended up with him. I felt if I just

disappeared, it would be easier for everyone. I'm so sorry for your loss of such a beautiful person. We should talk sometime. My number is 971-357-8572.

–

I send out the invitations to the annual Christmas Eve drop-in, minus one this year for mom and Jim.

After the family drama with mom's siblings, me nor Marin have heard from them and we are now certain uncle Daniel started plotting against me during mom's illness to replace me in their Will. All mom's sibling knew how much money mom was worth. But mom never talked about her wealth with me. The only time she told me about how much money she made, was her last year at Xerox, before she retired, she said she had her best year and she made two hundred fifty-five thousand dollars.

Still, I am just trying to focus on Christmas, and trying to figure out how I can afford to buy presents for everyone again this year. I will charge everything on credit cards as usual. I just keep thinking that as soon as Sheldon graduates from Hoggard, I will sell the house and pay off all my debts and go rent an apartment somewhere.

Marin and her family arrive on the twenty-third and they all plan to go to Circular Church downtown for Christmas Eve service and then come to the party. Samantha comes home Christmas Eve morning. Her dorm at UNC-W is the only dorm building open during Holidays. With her part time work schedule, it is usually easier for her to stay in the dorm during her breaks. Sheldon doesn't have practice this week and is helping me out a lot around the house and sets up the garage for the party for the kids to play ping pong and darts and a golf hole game.

The annual party starts, and dozens of people arrive and everyone is eating and drinking and having a good time. There is one good thing I learned from my ex-husband, and that is how to entertain and throw a party. He taught me how to set up a food table, bar table, and garnish and plate food. All the teenagers are in the garage playing and my suspicion is they might be sneaking in beer and alcohol. My cell phone is on top of the refrigerator and I just happen to be standing close by and hear it ring around nine-thirty. I grab it and see it is Sharon calling from California. I start walking upstairs to take the call so I can hear her. 'Scarlet, I'm sorry to bother you on Christmas Eve but my cousin Casey called, and Jim went to visit her in New Mexico today and Jim told Casey he is filing a lawsuit against you for slander, for the email you sent to the Sunday School class. Someone forwarded the email to Jim'.

We continue chatting about how crazy he is, and I say I am not worried; one because I told the truth in my email, and two, I have no money for him to get, and three, what whacko attorney would take the case. Apparently, Jim and Uncle Daniel went to New Mexico together for the Holidays and it appears they are spending a lot of time together. Me and Sharon hang up and I go back downstairs and tell Marin. Marin is in disbelief, but she is not worried either.

The rest of the holidays were busy, spending time with friends and family and going to Marin's New Year's Eve party in her Shell Island home.

On Monday morning I decide to take a vacation day. I know my boss will be frustrated with me since I have taken so much time off with mom's illness, but I still need a break. The reality of mom's death still hasn't set in yet, with my anger at Jim, and disappointment with mom's siblings. Everything has taken a toll on me emotionally. I hear a knock at the door, and I peak through the transom window and see it is a tall, skinny, older man with gray hair, and I see a gold sedan parked in front of my house on the street. I open the door and this stranger gives me an envelope. He explained that he is a Constable serving me with legal papers. He walks away, I close the door, and I open the envelope:

New Hanover County of North Carolina
Plaintiff: Jim Reardon vs Defendant: Scarlet Gaines; Slander/Libel

The words are jumping out at me, *Jury Trial*. I feel like I am going to faint.

'Jim has filed the lawsuit against me. I was just served the legal papers,' I exclaim to Marin on the phone. She suggests I find an attorney right away and she assumes since I am so broke and poor I should qualify for a free public defender. She could be right. I start doing research online and go to the North Carolina Bar Association website and submit my inquiry online. A few hours later a woman calls from the organization and I explain my situation and the legal documents I was served. She tells me that Civil Cases are not eligible for free defense attorneys.

Me, dad, and Marin conference call each other in disbelief that this is actually happening. How can a man be so crazy? How could a person be so mean and hateful?

Via google.com Edward Phillips pops up as reputable and I call his office and schedule an appointment for Tuesday afternoon at two o'clock.

Next, I pull out my insurance card and look for the Employee Assistance info and call the toll-free number to find another counselor. I am shaking as I continue to be in a state of shock.

The lady on the other end says she will connect me with Meg Talbot in Seagate and schedules me an appointment for Thursday.

Chapter 14: Go Fund Me

It is a crisp cool day in downtown Wilmington, and I get lucky and find a side street parking spot on Broad Street. It is difficult for me to walk down the cobblestone street in my two-inch high heels, but I manage to get on the sidewalk and walk upstairs in the old historic building to the Law office. The receptionist greets me and guides me to the conference room that looks like a library with books aligned in bookcases on three sides of the walls. She hands me a bottled water, a legal pad, and there are six pens laying on the table. Five minutes later Mr. Phillips walks in and sits down across from me. I explain the events of my mom's illness, the abuse of my stepfather, and show him the legal Summons. He tells me that Slander cases are the hottest cases in North Carolina right now, and that numerous awards are being won, but with few collections. He continues to jabber on and on about his success and how the legal system works and the process, to the point that I see through his arrogance and it appears he likes to hear himself talk. Then he tells me he would need a thirty-thousand dollars retainer fee upfront. Trying not to pass out, I simply tell him there is no way, and I had already explained to him I have no money and that I am a struggling divorced mom trying to make ends meet each month. Basically, I tell him thanks but no thanks, and he tells me this case will be a minimum of fifty thousand dollars regardless of the attorney I retain. There is no possible way for me to come up with that amount of money.

Quickly I get out of that office and practically run to the car, trying not to fall down, and I call Marin. 'What? Thirty-five thousand dollars? Fifty thousand dollars?' She advises for me to keep looking and to schedule consultations with other attorneys. I go back to work for a remaining hour and half and I can't concentrate. Looking online I find two other law firms to contact and schedule appointments with one on Thursday morning and one of Friday afternoon.

My meeting with attorney Chris Landrum is good and he seems pleasant and he tells me I would need to contact Verizon to obtain all the old text messages on my phone to retrieve for evidence in my defense. He asks for a five thousand retainer fee upfront to handle the case and he confirms what Edward Phillips said about a minimum of fifty thousand dollars in total fees. He mentions I may want to call my homeowner's insurance agency, State Farm to see if I have insurance coverage that may cover my legal services.

When I get home, I call the local State Farm office and they give me a corporate number to call. The girl on the other ended sounded as if she couldn't be more than twenty years old. I explain my problem, she asks, 'Is this story for real? Is he crazy?'. Then I confirm this ordeal is factual and she is in disbelief. She tells me I do not have an umbrella policy and she will have the local agent Jack Tandem call me to explain. I start thinking at that moment, that I might need to set up a Go Fund Me account. I am going to need help from others.

On Friday morning I cross the Church Creek bridge to go to Pender Island to drive to the McGough Law firm. The receptionist Ashley is about thirty years old and looks like a model. She takes me the small conference room and there are several legal pads and pens on the table. Jason McGough walks in and he looks like he is in his late thirties. He sounds intellectual and you can tell he is very smart and well-educated, but I guess most attorneys are. I tell him the whole story and he reviews the Summons and Complaint, and he asks if everything I said in the email was true. And I say 'absolutely'. He asks how I can defend my statements in the email, and I tell him that I have hundreds and hundreds of text messages and emails with mom's friends and family bashing Jim and complaining about his abuse towards her. He informs me there is an app I can download on my iPhone to retrieve all the old text messages and then he can download them on his computer. Jason tells me he is surprised that nationally known attorney Fred Cason took this case knowing I have no money. Fred won a prestigious lawsuit against BMW for a bad paint job in Alabama in the early nineties. 'Jim's attorney is a bully and because you have no money, he will go after your house. North Carolina law allows up to a one hundred thousand dollars exemption. Because you have over one hundred thousand dollars of Equity in your home, that it is the reward he is going after if Jim wins the case. All he needs is one jury to believe your statements were false. But Jim will have to prove he suffered some loss as a result of your email. The definition of slander is making a false statement to cause harm.' I am thinking Jason is the one I need to hire, and he too wants a five thousand retainer fee. I ask if I can set up a Go Fund Me page to raise money for my legal fees, and he agrees that is a good idea and he will approve the verbiage before I set it up the internet account.

I tell him Marin is worried about Daniel being able to file a lawsuit against me since I mentioned his arrest and criminal record in my email. Jason reassures me there is nothing Daniel can do, since his legal troubles were public knowledge and printed in the newspaper and televised in the news media.

'What about the Jewelry that Jim refuses to give to my daughter that my mom legally and rightfully left for Samantha? There has to be some legal way to get the jewelry.'

He replies 'Yes, but you will need to contact a Probate attorney. We will refer you to the Kuhn & Kuhn Law Firm. You will need to call them to discuss your options.'

Jason wants me to go to the Probate Office downtown and get a copy of mom's Probate file so he can know how much mom and Jim were worth, and how much money Jim has to spend on attorney fees. He says that if I win at trial, with my counter claims, I can be reimbursed my attorney fees and all my counseling sessions. He asks me to put together a list of scriptures about being a man of God, to confirm what the bible says about acting like a man of God.

He explains the three counter claims that he will file: Abuse of Process, Frivolous Proceedings, Malicious Prosecution. Abuse of Process is the use of the process to coerce or extort that is the abuse and need not be accompanied by any ill will.

The North   Carolina
Frivolous Civil Proceedings Sanction Act provides for liability for attorney fees and costs of frivolous suits. ... believes, as an attorney of record, in good faith that his procurement, initiation, continuation, or defense of a civil cause is not intended to merely harass or injure the other party.
Malicious Prosecution is Under North Carolina law, a person who has been the subject of criminal prosecution without probable cause or a baseless lawsuit may have a civil cause of action against the person or entity that instituted the proceedings.

Jason also would like me to go ahead and get statements from the people that will support me and can back up my email to the Sunday School class; "We need to go ahead and get an email statement from all of them, in case they die. It will be too expensive to get depositions from all these people'.

We decide to get statements from Kate Mulvaney, Bethany Miller, and Jim's daughter Sharon, Kathy Denlinger and Cathy Hillrom, and the Girdwood's; all the people willing to testify on my behalf. Kate was one of mom's closest friends from their Xerox days. They worked together in Raleigh and they both transferred to the North Virginia office in the same year. Kate still works there today, and she travels the country in the National Sales division. She has never remarried despite being absolutely beautiful in her early sixties. She says she will give a statement regarding the visit she had with mom two months before she died and the conversation they had. Mom told Kate she admired her for never remarrying because she settled by staying married to Jim. Mom also told Kate her concerns about the Will, and Kate tried to tell mom that it was ridiculous because it is all mom's money.

Kathy and Cathy both never married, and mom met them in nineteen eighty-two when she moved to Raleigh. They were her neighbors in her apartment complex; they lived directly across on the first floor. Kathy eventually moved and settled in Charlotte and Cathy moved to Northern Virginia and still spent a lot of time with mom after she moved up there. They all have known Jim since he came in mom's life and they all knew how mom kept so many secrets from him.
Greg and Gayle Girdwood are outraged by the lawsuit and eagerly want to give a statement about the conversation mom had with them just weeks before she passed.

Bethany is trying to hold on to her life to live long enough to give her statement as she continues to struggle with major health problems. She says that is her motivation for staying alive, being a witness for me.

But Jason determines that a deposition will be necessary from Louanne since she was aware about all the abuse and she was sending me the majority of texts messages and emails about mom and how Jim was treating her. Louanne will be my strongest witness.

Jason helps downloads the app on my iPhone at the end of our meeting and he immediately downloads all my text messages on his computer. All the group text messages from Louanne, Marin, June, Daniel, Johnny, Lindsey, and Libba. The PDF file is over three hundred pages.

I walk out of his office with a slight sense of relief. Jason really knows what he is doing, and he is the right attorney to help me. I just need to figure out where I am going to get the money from for these legal fees and I hope I can raise enough from Go Fund Me.

It is now after five o'clock and I get caught in the afternoon traffic on the Forden Bridge. At least the sun is shining, and I can admire the glistening water on the Cape Fear River as it takes me at least ten minutes to get across the beautiful structure. I finally get home and Sheldon is not around; he is at basketball practice, I think. Then I call Marin and she doesn't answer, so I call dad and in his usually positive voice chimes 'the Lord is going to handle this', and he is certain Jim will come to his senses and drop the case. 'Dad, he has the audacity to file the case, he will go through with it, this lawsuit gives him a reason to live'.

Marin calls back and she agrees the idea to start a Go Fund Me page to raise money for my attorney fees. I tell her that Aunt

Paula has already said she was going to contact the Ellen Show. She too is hopeful that this story is going to get national news exposure somehow.

Jim's daughter Sharon emails her statement the day after I ask her   for   it:
The words that come to mind describing my dad are angry, controlling, critical, demeaning, negative, and harsh. I left home at seventeen and didn't want to ever see him again. When I told him, I was leaving he asked I how intended on taking care of my family. I told him at least they will have love. He then said in a demeaning tone, "how are you going to buy food with love, how are you going to pay utilities with love, etc.". I didn't even want to go to college because that would mean I would still have to go back for holidays and summer. I moved out and then to Florida for five years, to New Mexico for few years and then to California.

My parents had a horrible marriage. My dad was in the Army, so we were constantly moving; California, Japan, Virginia, Florida, Virginia again. There was never any display of affection of any kind or even a civil conversation, always berating. My mother had no support from friends and family so family didn't know how bad it was. When my grandmother came out to visit and saw urged my mom to leave. She left several times to go live with my father's mother whom he was also demeaning to until she finally left for good to live with her. I would hear my dad saying, "you're so stupid" so many times to my mother and ask her "when are you going to get out of my life". He was especially cruel to my brother Tony who suffered many beatings with a belt, one time with a bloody face after being hit in the face with braces. The worse part though was the emotional abuse. He would tell him how worthless he was and how would

130

never amount to anything. I recently asked my mom how many times she thought he was whipped with a belt and she said about a hundred. She said first time when about three and was at a neighborhood park in a swing and didn't come when called and he went out with a belt and whipped him. Tony was sent to live with grandmother last two years of high school. I started working at sixteen so I could have a car and enough money to leave. That was my only goal. I had very little self-confidence or any other aspiration.

I grew up extremely timid and shy. I would cry very easily. My early memories are one day sitting outside playing on a sidewalk and my dad came to find me for dinner. I had feet that turned inwards and had special inserts in my shoes. When my dad came to me my shoes were off and the inserts were missing. He started yelling and grabbed me by one arm and hitting me on the way home. I remember looking at the fried chicken my mom had made which was my favorite but too upset to eat. I think I was about four. When we were in Japan, my dad woke me up in the middle of the night. He was yelling that they were getting a divorce and asked who I wanted to live with. I was crying as usual and said both of them because I was afraid what my dad would do if I said my mom. I found out after Tony died that he had told his girlfriend that story and when they brought him in he said "neither of you". Another time on Christmas Day that he had us come straight for a talk before celebrating Christmas just to say "we're getting a divorce" which was nothing new but seemed like wanted to make sure to hurt my mom by ruining our Christmas. I often felt he was mean to us to get to her.

Tony went on to become an alcoholic and compulsive liar. He had many failed relationships and was arrested for assaulting a girlfriend and ordered to attend Alcoholics Anonymous and was allowed to work during week and spend weekends in jail. Through AA he was able to turn his life around and worked with a life couch named Nancy. He was diagnosed with Hepatitis C about fifteen years ago. I asked him when he used needles and said he was using heroin in high school while living with grandmother. He also told me that he was an alcoholic at twelve years of age. That he drank every day from my dad's bar downstairs when we were in Florida.

He drowned scuba diving in October, two thousand five. He had an injection of interferon the night before going out to Coronado Island for nighttime lobster diving. I talked to him the night before I asked if he felt safe doing that because he had been so weakened from the interferon. He said would be fine, was only eighteen feet of water and he would not be reaching his hand into the hole to pull out the lobster. I received a call the next day that Tony had drowned and was devastating. Tony and I had never talked about our childhood.

The next week was going up to La Jolla Beach where he lived and having to plan and put together funeral and memorial. My dad and Glenna were there too. One day my dad was sitting at the beach and said he was upset that Tony didn't leave him anything in his Will, only my mother. I told him he didn't deserve any of it and walked away. My grief got worse and worse after the funeral and was not functioning well. I decided I'd better go for help and went to a grief counselor. She asked me to write letters to family members and bring back to her. My letter to my dad was full of hatred, blaming him for Tony's death in an inadvertent way. If he hadn't been so abusive Tony would have never been a heroin user and then been on interferon. Tony was very strong athletically and should have been able to get himself out of whatever happened that night. The therapist told me that I would be stuck in grief if I didn't get rid of that anger. She said I would need to forgive him so I could move through the grief process. He came out and met with her also, she confronted him with the abuse, and she told him "Mr. Reardon, you did in fact abuse your son whipping with a belt". He apologized and after that started having more contact again.

About the time Glenna was having her first surgery. my dad called berating me for not being out east for Glenna, she has two daughters and tons of friends and family. I hung up on him and felt I can't let him get to me again and didn't want to have any more contact with him. I went to a counselor because it set me back in fight or flight where I couldn't concentrate, I kept having flashbacks of my childhood and my dad's angry demeanor. I decided I needed help again and after one visit with the counselor she described him as been narcissistic and had me read a book called "The Seven Deadly Sins of Narcissism". It described him perfectly. We had about twelve more sessions and she agreed that ending the relationship may be the best because with his personality disorder he will never see he is in the wrong, there is lack of insight that ordinary people possess. My dad and I had a couple more conversations that turned nasty and then I said why don't we just end this all right now and he said fine and that was it, that was about two years ago. I don't want to ever see him again.

I ended up with all of Tony's things after he died, and he liked to write things down. He had books that he wrote in the columns and would highlight. He struggled in relationships and he had Deepak Chopra "Love". There was a comment about not being able to love if numb inside that he had highlighted with stars at the side. His girlfriend had tried to take him to counseling and he walked out when asked about his childhood. He had comments written different places "unable to love" also "unable to look up to his dad". I had his phone, so I had to let everyone know about his death. One of them was Nancy, the life coach he started with. She said the remarkable thing about Tony was that he didn't know what a feeling was. She asked him how he was feeling and said didn't have feelings. She continued to have contact with him for a few years. Tony also went on a retreat in Hawaii that was an intimacy workshop to work on feeling. He had many writings about that and Sissy, the girlfriend that loved him but Tony couldn't make the connection. His comment about me was that we were both in our cocoons which was correct. I have a hard time with affection too and my husband has been understanding.

I had thought that maybe my dad had changed with Glenna but apparently not. She was a very sweet lady. I feel so bad that my dad has now disowned Scarlet.

I call the Kuhn & Kuhn law firm and leave a voice message. Hours later Augusta Kuhn returns my call. I tell her about the Will leaving the jewelry to my daughter, and she said she can help but the retainer fee required is five thousand dollars. 'That won't make sense because we don't know what jewelry mom had left in her jewelry box and it is doubtful the jewelry is worth that much'. Me and Marin think there were probably on a few gold bracelets and a few pairs of gold earrings, and some costume jewelry items. I call Marin and she agrees 'It doesn't make sense because the jewelry left in her jewelry box probably isn't worth more than one thousand dollars. Maybe you can get it when you go to trial, maybe the judge can demand Jim give the jewelry to Samantha. I can't comprehend why any juror would ever side with him. Can you imagine what the jury will think when they hear all the reasons why he disowned you, 'you stroked your daughter's hair, you ate M&M's out of a bowl, he didn't like the food you brought over from Baja Tower. Seriously, I think it is best you go to trial because maybe the jury will award you the amount of money in mom's Will and the value of her estate, if you win the Counterclaims. Rich agrees with me and he thinks this whole lawsuit is going to make Jim look like the true narcissist he is.'

I go to the Go Fund Me website and create an account and type in my post:

My mother, Glenna Reardon, passed away on November eighteenth as she lost her battle to peritoneal cancer after seventeen months of suffering. I was by her side for countless doctor's appointments, twelve chemo treatments, six surgeries, multiple Emergency Room visits, etc. One week after she passed, on Thanksgiving Day my stepfather, Jim Reardon, cut me and my children out of his life for no good reason. I had to tell my kids that Jim did not want to be their Grandpa anymore, their Grandpa since their birth. The following Sunday, I emailed members of his church asking to pray for him and to pray for me to forgive him. I informed them of the situation, honestly, and how he treated my mother during her illness. Now, he has filed a civil lawsuit against me, with a requested jury trial, for slander/libel. I can say with confidence that my statements in the email were factual and justifiable. Unfortunately, it is going to cost me about fifty thousand dollars in attorney fees to defend these frivolous and untrue allegations. Civil cases are not eligible for Pro Bono assistance and I have exhausted all efforts for free legal help, including filing a Liability Claim with my State Farm Homeowners, but I do not have a Personal Umbrella Policy. His attorney recently notified my attorney that Jim will not drop the case. As a struggling single mother of two kids (one who is in college and both enrolled in Medicaid) and no assets other than my house, I am in desperate need of financial assistance to continue with this case. My stepfather is persecuting me and I am in danger of losing my home. My mother was a wonderful person who loved her two daughters and four grandchildren more than anything. They say there are no tears in heaven, but I am certain my mom is crying harder now than she ever did while on this earth as she watches her daughter struggle with this undeserved pain and stress.

Marin comes up with the idea to contact some Women's Rights Organizations or Christian groups that may be willing to donate funds. I google Women's Right Organizations and find numerous ones listed on a Wikipedia page. I click on each of the links to determine what the mission is for each organization and decide to contact MIAMOMS, Concerned Women for America, National American for Women Suffrage, NOW, Royal Neighbors of America, Ladies of Liberty Alliance. I copy and paste the Go Fund Me posting and alter the verbiage slightly and I send emails to these six groups. Maybe I will get some responses.

The donations are coming in from the Go Fund Me account. I get an email notification with each donation. Some are anonymous, dozens are small amounts like twenty dollars, many at fifty dollars, and one large donation at one thousand, and some at several hundred dollars. The total raised in one week is about five thousand which is what I need for the retainer fee. 'Thank you, dear Jesus!' Now I need to figure out how to raise forty-five thousand dollars.

I go meet with Jason again, and I have done my homework, as he calls it, as I had printed all the text messages and emails and organized them in a binder with over three hundred pages included. He also had me draft my 'answer' to the summons and I use the references in the binder.

"Boy, you have done a lot of work. This is extremely organized and makes my job easier. Good Job!'

It took over five hours to accomplish this task, printing all the emails from my sent items, separating the text messages pages from the email pages by month, labeling each page at the bottom if it was Text or Email and the month, and put in order by date, and using divider tabs in the binder to separate them.

I give him a copy of the probate file, it's twenty-three pages and it cost me twenty dollars at the courthouse to retain it. He reviews the file, and we discuss that fact that mom's estate is worth over two million dollars. It is no wonder Daniel plotted against me, if his plan works, he will inherit all of it. "Well, Jim does have plenty of money to waste on attorney fees", Jason states.

I tell him that my sister wants me to ask about a Restraining Order against Jim. My counselor Meg is also worried that he could harm me and my children, and she too believes I need a Restraining Order. Meg tells me that his narcissist personality type is capable of hurting others, and not himself. But Jason says I don't have enough proof that he would physically hurt me and the kids because he hasn't made any threats to do so. Marin even thinks Daniel is a threat. Marin worries that it could be possible for Daniel to kill Jim and try to frame me, because he is going to do anything and everything to make sure he inherits all of mom's money. An eerie feeling comes over me, with a sensation that I may be looking over my shoulder as long as Jim and Daniel are alive on this earth.

Before I leave, I write him a check for five thousand dollars for the retainer fee, and I ask him if I can email the people in the Sunday School class for financial help and he says that will be fine; 'yes, good idea'.

Chapter 15: Hypocrites

I send an email to the church people asking for help with legal fees; Jason drafts the email for me, and the verbiage is similar to the Go Fund Me page. Immediately, I receive a reply from Trish Ellis.

'There you go again. We are fully supporting Jim.'

I forward to Marin and she replies 'who is that'. I respond 'she is a friend of mom's, they aren't that close, she brought over dinner once while she was sick.

Then I get another one from Bill Schmidt; 'I will pray for you and Jim'. I have no idea who this Bill is.

None of mom's closest church friends respond; Lindsey, Libba or Maryann. Me nor Marin have heard from any of them since mom died.

I am feeling so bewildered, because I cannot understand how anyone could support Jim in any capacity.

It's almost spring, and the birds are chirping out my bedroom window. I am half-awake already when the alarm goes off and I roll out of bed ready to muddle through another work week. After getting ready, I go downstairs and make breakfast burritos for Sheldon. I tell him there is a frozen lasagna thawing in the fridge for him to bake for his dinner since I am going to Bible Study Fellowship tonight as it resumes again from the holiday break. I leave my phone in the car during the bible study as I don't like to get distracted and I prefer to focus on the Lord for two hours. BSF has been important to me since nineteen ninety-two when I began the program living in Charlotte after college, and it is one reason I stayed married for so long. The international program strongly discourages divorce, rightfully so, because God is very clear in the bible 'I hate divorce'. It is a big commitment for me since it meets at Grace on The River Church in Monkey Junction, which is about twenty miles from my home.

I get in the car to leave the church parking lot and I have a missed call from Marin and a text message:

Call me as soon as you can

'I just got out of bible study, what's up?'

"Rich got a call from his parents, and Jim forwarded your email to them, and Jim called them, and it appears Doug Hibben is the one that forwarded the email to Jim. Rich's dad asked if everything in the email as true, and Rich told them 'yes, all of it'. Jim told Rich's dad that most everyone in the church is supporting him in his lawsuit against you'.
Me: 'Well, that Doug Hibben is the biggest hypocrite and most every neighbor on the street despises him. And I have a hard time believing people in the church are supporting him. His lawsuit against me is not Christian'.

Marin: "Yes, and if Jim is forwarding the email to people, then is he slandering himself?'

Me: "Good point, I will mention to Jason when I meet with him this week'"

My meeting with Jason involves having him updating me on the legal documents he has filed at the courthouse. He tells me

about Jim's deposition last week 'We should receive the transcript of Jim's deposition soon. I think you will be delighted with how well that deposition went for you. I would like to wait and read it as it is tough to recall everything said during a deposition when you're taking it, but I believe the transcript will support a motion for summary judgment; asking the Court to rule in your favor without a trial because there are no facts in question, and you are entitled to judgment as a matter of law. I am certain the transcript will at least support a motion for partial summary judgment, excluding at least of portion of Jim's claims. We will evaluate that when we get the transcript.'
Eventually, he wants to subpoena the emails between my uncle Daniel and Jim, but Jason has it in his mind that eventually Jim will come to his senses and drop this case. I keep telling him that is not going to happen.

Next week the email arrives in my inbox and I click the link with the password and download the two hundred and eight pages of Jim's deposition. Before I open the PDF to read it, I forward it to dad and Marin because Jason says it is public information and I can send it to anyone. It is disheartening to read. Jim does admit he didn't want my mom to have Hospice care, he admits to taking mom to all those places while she was so sick. Then he says the goal of the lawsuit is to be rewarded with money from me to give to the church. He wants a minimum of one hundred thousand dollars to be split between Seaside Baptist Church and CoastalLife Community Church.
Hours later, dad calling; "boy, your attorney sure did a good job handling Jim, he earned his money for those two hours"

Me: 'yeah, but did you see all the men in the church he listed as supporting him? Old rich white men trying to take my home away from me.'

Dad- 'the Lord will deal with them. The bible specifically discusses hypocrites in the church.'

But deep down, I still don't believe it and I think Jim is lying about all those church people supporting him. I am thinking he has the onset of dementia and that he is delirious.

Me and Sheldon decide to go the eleven o'clock service, since that is the usual service we attend, even though we know it will be the most crowded for this Easter Sunday. We have been attending CoastalLife Community Church since inception, the spin off church of Seaside Baptist we previously attended. We each get our coffee from the coffee bar and sit on the second to last row. After the three praise and worship songs, Chip begins his sermon. He is preaching about having a path in life and how to have faith in times of trouble. Then I can't believe my ears; I look over at Sheldon and say 'that's Jim, he is talking about Jim'. Gosh, Chip Morris is a pastor, he is supposed to be a servant of God, he is supposed to follow Christ, and he is supporting the man trying to make me homeless in the pulpit! He is supporting Jim with me and my son sitting in the congregation!

Chip- 'my friend Jim lost his wife in last November to cancer. They were married for twenty-six years. He came to my office this week for prayer and comfort. He tells me that he goes to bed every night crying and he wakes up every morning crying' then I just tune out the rest of his sermon as he is praising Jim Reardon, calling him his friend and I say to Sheldon 'Let's get the hell out of here' and we dart up from the blue classroom chairs and storm out the closed double doors. I don't think I will ever attend another Southern Baptist Church service the rest of my life.

The stress of the legal fees is mounting. I take the Ziploc bag of jewelry mom gave me and the sterling silver flatware to

141

Wilmington Gold and Diamond located in the Belle Hall Shopping Center. The gold coin necklace surrounding by diamonds is worth over two thousand dollars. It is so unique and rare as mom had it custom made. She won the gold coin for her successful sales results at Xerox. It is the only piece of jewelry I ever wanted, and mom knew I would wear it. The salesclerk tells me mom's engagement ring Jim gave her is only worth nine hundred dollars because it is so outdated and not a popular cut. The gold bracelets and other few stone rings are worth several hundred dollars. The silver flatware is worth three hundred dollars. The total for everything is four thousand three hundred seventy-six dollars. The lady writes me a check and I deposit it on my phone via my Bank of America app. I write out a check to the McGough Law Firm as soon as I get back home and put in in my mailbox. I call Marin and I tell her I sold mom's jewelry and I don't know how I can come up with the rest of the funds needed for the lawsuit. 'Scarlet, don't worry, I will call Jason's office and give them my credit card and have them invoice me every month. Mom would want me to do this for you as she would be devastated if she had any idea what Jim and Daniel are putting you through. It is unbelievable that the church people are supporting him. They are true examples of hypocrites.' I hang up the phone and start crying, crying with relief that my sister is so generous; also crying because I feel like I am being persecuted by these church people.

Chapter 16: Betrayal

This has been a long year; meeting with the attorney frequently, the stress of the lawsuit, trying to pay my bills each month, busy with my job, waiting for Sheldon to graduate high school. I never would have thought a lawsuit could drag out for so long. My trial is probably months away, Jason tells me. I am ready for the Holidays and can't wait to see Marin and her family soon.

■■

Jason's office sends a pdf file of the emails he recently obtained between my uncle Daniel and Jim. He tells me that because of attorney client privilege I am not allowed to send them to anyone, but I violate that rule and I send to Dad and Marin anyway. It takes me over an hour to read the one hundred seventy-one pages. It's interesting, it is like Daniel is trying to brown nose Jim. They are traveling together, they have a trip planned to Cancun, New Mexico again, California and a big adventure to the Holy Land planned, and somehow Daniel convinced Jim to buy a lot on the golf course in Pinehurst, North Carolina. I guess that is where Daniel wants to retire, near Johnny and Sandy's house. Jim brags about how much wealth he has, that he is so solvent, he can waste money on the legal fees. Daniel is encouraging Jim to continue with the lawsuit. They both joke about replacing me in the Will and Daniel asks to borrow some money from Jim for Mike's new business venture. Mike has finally left the prestigious Bernhardt furniture company in Manhattan and has opened his own furniture store on Long Island. They discuss trying to find someone to testify on Jim's behalf. Daniel asks Jim if he thinks he can convince Louanne to be his witness for the lawsuit, and Jim says he isn't sure since she said all those bad things about him in her emails.

Then Jim writes that he thinks Lindsey Lawton will be a good witness because she still reaches out to Jim and they talk frequently at church. And Kit Wofford. Kit was more of a golf acquaintance of mom's as they played in the Member/Member golf tournament together at Landfall each year.

Dad and Darlene call after reading the emails. They usually call together, and dad puts the iPhone on speaker phone.

'Unbelievable. It's as if Daniel is courting Jim, as if it is a romantic relationship almost. It is hard to believe he would do this to you. I have known Daniel since he was a teenager. How could he do this to your mother?'.

Marin calls and says 'Daniel is going to spend all of mom's money before Jim dies, buying lots, traveling the world, funding Mike's new business venture. It is hard to believe mom could be so naïve. She would be so disgusted to know how her own brother betrayed her trust and plotted against her own daughter'. Marin is completely repulsed with Daniel's behavior. She tells me that she forgot to unfriend our cousin Miles on Facebook, and she saw one of his posts this week and she is pretty certain that Daniel is now living with Jim in mom's house. Miles was on vacation with his family in Wilmington and shared a picture of them at Vickery's Restaurant on the waterway and June commented 'Daniel's favorite restaurant', and Miles replied 'Yes, we are visiting dad'.
'Why would Kit Wofford testify for Jim? I didn't know mom was that close to her. Have you ever met her?' Me: 'Yes, I met her a couple of times, but she didn't know any of the details about how Jim was treating mom as mom, and she didn't spend that much time with her. She did bring dinner over one night towards the end of mom's illness. Not sure she understands exactly what she has now gotten herself into.'

I send Jason a follow up email regarding my concerns with the emails between Jim and Daniel.

From: *Scarlet Gaines [mailto:scarletgaines@yahoo.com]*
Sent: *Tuesday, December 20, 2016 8:33 PM*
To: *Jason McGough jason@mcgoughawfirm.com*

Subject: *Re: Reardon v. Gaines*

Jason,
I read through most of it all last night and cannot stomach to look at it again. I was suspicious of Daniel hours after mom's death, and knew after all this went down, that he began plotting against me during mom's illness. It appears he plans on spending all of my mom's money, trips to Israel, California, Cancun, New Mexico, a lot purchase in Pinehurst, etc.

At this point, I think we should obtain my mom's medical records which are over one thousand pages and will cost five hundred dollars from Novant Hospital. I will send you all the doctor visit recordings I have which include every visit except Dr. Holtz because none of us went with them to see her because we saw no point in mom going to her because she was a Primary Care Physician, and she is the one that gave mom a B12 shot two days before her death which the Hospice nurse did not approve. It's interesting that I have three hundred pages of emails and texts in which Daniel was included in during my mom's illness and he never responded to one; yet he can send Jim hundreds of emails.

Also, is it legal for him to continue to send copies of my three hundred pages of evidence he calls The Book?

Here are some of my notes:

* email 4/26/16 - why has nobody ever mentioned Jim's decision to disown me and my children and the comments and lies he made about us?
* email 5/1/16 - what is Jim leaving Johnny Ledford in his Will?
* email 6/12/16 - he can't believe I kept all the emails/texts. Duh, it's called modern technology and all items stay in my sent folder, and my smart attorney had the app to download all prior text messages.
* email 7/18/16 - Jim says Daniel is the only one that stood up for him; yes, because Daniel wants all the money, the house, and the car.
* email 7/27/16 - what three of my witnesses is he referring to? How can his lawyer be pleased with his homework?
* email 8/1/16 - not sure why Daniel hopes it goes to court soon cause his homosexual ass will be on the stand too.
* email 8/3/16 - "Glenna was/is my everything and she would want me to do these together with you". Uh, Glenna is rolling over in her grave and several of my witnesses will testify how she worried how he would treat me, their disagreements over the Will, etc. My mom told him she would 'haunt him from the grave'.
* email 8/31/16 - Dr. Holtz will need to answer why she gave my mother bloodwork and a B12 shot while under Hospice care and two days before she died. Hospice nurse can discuss.

*email 8/29/16 - that I will be sorry I put June down as a witness. Well, June will have to tell the truth about her emails and statements. June is a piece of work, and most people consider her different; and I am being nice. June also knew about mom's secrets from Jim; hidden money, etc. She had said she would never see Jim again after mom died, so why is she his witness?

* email 10/3/16 - why would Fred Cason meet with Daniel Ledford just to talk.

I talked to my mom's best friend Bethany today and she is willing to do whatever it takes on my behalf because Jim's was so 'shitty' to my mom, her words. She has a new address: 4005 Grand Rockville Way, #312, Raleigh, NC 27571.

I am willing to drive to Raleigh to get her and bring her back for deposition if necessary.

Do you have to respond or comment on these emails?

Email from Jason:
RE: Reardon v. Gaines

- **Jason McGough <jason@mcgoughlaw.com>**

  Scarlet,

  I agree with your concerns. It appears that Daniel is manipulating Jim for personal financial gain. It also appears he is a primary force behind Jim's decision to sue you and to continue prosecuting this case.

Jim is obviously cherishing how "solvent" his estate it and is spending the money however he wishes, including maliciously prosecuting you in this action and "rewarding" Daniel for his "loyalty". This dynamic is problematic because we now know that Fred Cason is representing Jim on a billable hour basis, which answers your question(s) about why Fred would meet with Daniel and has met with Jim so many times (Fred is financially incentivized to spend time "working" on Jim's case and is being compensated for these meetings).

Likewise, Fred is being compensated to continue prosecuting the case, regardless of the outcome (which would not be the case if his representation were based on a contingency – where he would not get paid unless and until he got Jim some money for the claims). For example, a trial will/would likely cost each side in excess of an additional twenty thousand dollars for attorney fees. Jim appears ready, willing and able to invest that kind of money in prosecuting you even though he acknowledged that he does not expect to receive any money from you in the end. This makes the objective of settling the case very difficult because Jim's primary objective appears to be harming you and having his "day in Court" no matter the anticipated result.

Jim does disclose some attorney-client privileged information to Daniel. Apparently, if Jim's recount to Daniel is accurate, Fred intends to make a motion to dismiss your counterclaims against Jim (malicious prosecution, abuse of process and violation of frivolous proceedings act) at the start of trial. Such a motion would only be successful if we had/have no evidence supporting the counterclaims. We already have some such information and evidence (that Jim is doing this maliciously and for some other ulterior purpose). We will likely gain significantly more evidence when we depose Daniel (which has become a necessity given the documentation produced).

The documents produced by Daniel have been sent to Fred Cason (required under the Rules). I believe these documents will further erode Fred's confidence in his client and the claims against you. However, Fred is a lawyer, and he will not likely disclose this reality to us. Attorneys have an ethical duty to zealously represent a client, even if they do not personally believe in their clients' claims or position. So, regardless of whether Fred's personal opinion of Jim or his claims evolves, Fred will continue prosecuting the case unless and until Jim changes his mind.

If you want to discuss all or any of this, please give me a call. I will be in the office today and tomorrow but will be on vacation next week for the Holidays and will return to the office on January 3.

If I don't talk to you this week, please try to push all of this out of your mind. Regardless of whether we talk this week, you've had a rough year, and you deserve to find some way to have a break from the stress and anxiety. So, your primary homework assignment for the next few weeks is to enjoy yourself and have a Merry Christmas!
Jason

Chapter 17: Perjury Problem

This year continues to be full of anxiety, meeting with the attorney frequently, the continued stress of the lawsuit, trying to pay my bills each month, busy with my job. I never would have thought a lawsuit could drag out for so long. I am ready for Sheldon's graduation and I am so excited for him and his future. The scholarship offers kept coming in through the first of April and he decided to play basketball for Barton College.

•••

Marin and Rich and the boys flew in this morning for the Senior banquet tonight. Dad and Darlene get to my house about four o'clock and we all follow each other in two cars to the school. The Friday five o'clock traffic is not too bad today.

The banquet is catered by Hamby's, one of Wilmington's premier catering companies. It is a pretty fancy banquet, with all the tables decorated with ornate artwork designed by the students, and the buffet has grilled halibut, chicken, crab-cakes, steak kabobs, pasta salad, sweet potatoes, roasted vegetables, and assortment of breads and desserts. It is no surprise when Sheldon is named Athlete of the Year and I am beaming with pride. I feel a slight sense of relief knowing he made it through, and some-how I have made it through and was able to hang on to the house. That has been my goal since the divorce, to stay in the house until Sheldon graduated. And now I can't sell it, because Jim could get all the equity if I do.

After the banquet, we all go back to the house to open the graduation gifts. Darlene had bought pictures from the Basketball State Championship tournament and had a big collage framed picture made from the sporting event where

Sheldon was named Most Valuable Player. Marin and Rich give him two hundred dollars in a card, and I had his school basketball jersey framed in a large wooden shadow box.

Dad and Darlene leave to go back to Myrtle Beach and I just pray they don't hit any deer along highway seventeen. They don't usually drive at night and it's so late.

Sheldon leaves to go hang out with his girlfriend Jayda to celebrate while Larry and Bill are playing ping pong in the garage. I open a bottle of red wine and pour a glass for me, Marin, and Rich. Marin asks, 'did you read Louanne's deposition?'

Me- 'No, I figured I didn't need to, it is what it is, the truth is the truth, and I don't have the spare hour to read through hundreds of pages'

Marin- 'me either, I figured there is no need to read it.'

Jason's office had emailed the transcript earlier in the week and I just forwarded the email to dad and Marin and they never downloaded it either.

The Oakley family leaves Sunday morning and me and the kids agree to have a family dinner tonight for a change. Now that I don't go to church on Sundays anymore, I spend the morning walking three miles and then go to the grocery store to buy items to prepare for dinner.

On Wednesday during lunch time, my phone buzzes while I have it on silent sitting at my desk.
It is Jason calling; 'Scarlet, we have a problem, have you read Louanne's deposition?'

Me: "no, I figured I didn't need to'.

Jason: 'You need to read it, this is not good, she is Jim's witness. I tried to catch her in her own lies but she would recover well. We need to meet very soon to discuss the next strategy. Call my office and schedule a time for us to meet'.

Feeling baffled, I text Dad and Marin:

> My attorney called and he said I need to read Louanne's deposition, that she is Jim's witness.
> Dad: OK
> Marin: I will read it tonight.

I just cannot believe what I am reading. Louanne is taking Jim's side, she is lying, saying mom is the one that didn't want to wear the Depends, lying and saying mom wanted to go all those places. Jason asks her why she sent all the emails saying Jim is fucking crazy and she said she was just frustrated.

I start drinking Woodbridge Pinot Grigio, a big bottle I got at the store yesterday. My anger inside is something I have never felt before. Marin calls and she figures out that I am very intoxicated. I don't even know what I am saying. I am crying hysterically.

Me: 'How could she do this? How could she do this to my mother? She is lying, she lied under oath, that's perjury, that's a federal offense.

Marin tries to console me, unsuccessfully. I can't even think straight. I don't even know what time it is.

After we hang up, I throw the empty wine bottle against the kitchen cabinet and the glass shatters. I just leave the broken glass on the floor every-where and I go to bed and close my bedroom door. I start vomiting and make about five trips to the toilet and eventually fall asleep naked. I never even bother to text Sheldon or think to find out where he is or when he is coming home.

The dog is barking, and it sounds like she is on the screen porch. 'Sheldon, get the dog', I yell. No reply, no answer. The dog continues to bark for several more minutes and I finally put on my white terrycloth bathrobe and go downstairs. There is my dad sitting at my kitchen table. He is not an animal lover and he put Lily on the back porch and locked her in with the doggie gate. I ask, 'Where is Sheldon' and dad says he went to work. Dad tells me to take a shower then we will go to lunch. It is already one o'clock, that is how late I slept, that is how hungover I am. The hot water feels exhilarating and I put on a little bit of foundation make-up, dry my hair, and we leave to head out to find a place to eat. I decide on Dockside's because dad has never been there and it's a pretty day and we can sit outside by the water.

Dad gives me a lecture during lunch that I have to remain strong in faith in the Lord and the He will prevail, and He will take care of this. Dad makes me promise I will get an emergency counseling session with Meg.

Knowing I survived the night, dad comforts me, and he leaves to go back to Myrtle Beach after he drops me off in the driveway from the late lunch. I feel so fortunate to have a father that lives such a Christlike life.

Meg schedules me for eleven o'clock tomorrow, which gives me time to squeeze in her session before my meeting with Jason at two o'clock. I tell her all about Louanne's perjury in her deposition, with tears streaming down my face I ask, 'Is the Pastor going to lie?'. Meg says 'You need to be prepared for that. You need to be prepared for any church friend or church member to lie. Most of them have already given you reason to believe they are not true Christians, and they are all capable of lying.'

Meg continues: 'I think it is time you begin taking medication to handle the stress and anxiety. There is a portion of The Diagnostic and Statistical Manual of Mental Disorders, under the Post Traumatic Stress Disorder, called Post Traumatic Grief Disorder' which you are suffering from.'

She explains it is extremely difficult to recover from PTSD, and she tells me that it is her opinion that I will never be able to fully recover from all this and she recommends for me to undergo hypnosis after the trial, to erase all memories of my mother, erase the memories of the lawsuit. She asks me to schedule a psychiatric appointment with Dr. Furman to get a prescription for Trazadone. His office is in the suite next door to hers. She thinks the medication will also help with the insomnia the stress has caused me. I have only been sleeping four hours per night since being served legal papers when this nightmare began.

My meeting with Jason is at two o'clock and he is punctual as always. We meet in his conference room and he tells me one option is that we can file a 'third party lawsuit' against Louanne. Because I got the information from Louanne about how Jim treated mom in writing in her emails and her text messages, I can sue her so the money Jim wants from me for the church can now come from Louanne.

This is good news to my ears, because now I am thinking I can sell the house and get out of debt. Now the church and Jim can't get my home and now they can take the money from Louanne.

Marin and Rich both agree that Jason's strategy is good and it is exactly what that liar Louanne deserves.

Chapter 18: Anger Adjustment

Every day I awake, and I feel nothing but anger; mostly I am angry with my mother for leaving this mess. She was worried something would happen, yet she did nothing to protect me. Sunday morning comes and I decide since I longer believe in the church universal, I need to find a way to stay spiritually connected to the Lord. Not sure where I got the book from, but I find Priscilla Shirer's 'The Armor of God' in a stack of books in the linen closet. My coffee from the Keurig is piping hot and I plop down on the couch with a cup and the book. Maybe staying close to the Lord will help with my anger.

The Whole Armor of God Ephesians Chapter 6

Finally, be strong in the Lord and in the strength of his might. Put on the whole armor of God, that you may be able to stand against the schemes of the devil. For we do not wrestle against flesh and blood, but against the rulers, against the authorities, against the cosmic powers over this present darkness, against the spiritual forces of evil in the heavenly places. Therefore, take up the whole armor of God, that you may be able to withstand in the evil day, and having done all, to stand firm. Stand therefore, having fastened on the belt of truth, and having put on the breastplate of righteousness, and, as shoes for your feet, having put on the readiness given by the gospel of peace. In all circumstances take up the shield of faith, with which you can extinguish all the flaming darts of the evil one; and take the helmet of salvation, and the sword of the Spirit, which is the word of God.

Dad keeps telling me I am under attack from Satan. As I am reading, I tell myself that I will remain strong in my faith and study and memorize this scripture over the next few months until the trial begins. I will use this scripture during the trial.

The last two weeks of June I work on getting the house ready to put on the market; cleaning, purging, landscaping. The garage is overflowing with junk, so I clean it out again for the third time in three years since Stan moved out. I hire a handy man to do minor things like change out the screws in the windows, caulk in some areas, paint the baseboards downstairs, and fix Sheldon's closet doors.

My realtor friend Nora comes over and tells me she thinks I can list it for three hundred ninety-five thousand dollars. The housing market is hot in Seagate for homes under four hundred thousand, and with four true bedrooms and the large lot, she thinks it will sell quickly. With the July the fourth holiday approaching, she thinks it is best to list the house on the Multiple Listing Service the following week.

The 'for sale' sign goes in the yard on Friday, July seventh and the realtor app on my phone starts sounding off the next day with three showings scheduled already. The first offer comes through seven days later but it is contingent on the buyers selling their existing home in Ogden so I decline that offer. The next offer comes through on July twenty-first for ten thousand below my asking price and no contingencies. The buyers will be getting a VA loan which can be more time consuming with a slower closing date, but the date of Thursday, September seventh is noted on the real estate documents. We get that contract ratified in less than twenty-four hours. That was fast and I am so grateful I will be getting out of debt!

The next few weeks I am a busy beaver, trying to find a rental house knowing my credit score is too low to buy another home right now; knowing I need to rent for six months or a year to get out of debt and get through this lawsuit. Nora shows me a few properties for rent and I decide to cross the highway to rent in Dunes South. It is a three-bedroom two bath one story home with a garage and fenced backyard.

Since it is much smaller with less living space, I start listing furniture for sell on the Facebook Marketplace site. I need to sell my master bedroom set and the formal dining room set.

Closing day arrives and we sit for two hours in the closing attorneys conference room because there is an issue with the VA. Finally, we get the lending closing statement and my profit after fees and realtor fees is one hundred thirty-four thousand seven hundred eighty-eight dollars. But how quickly that money will begin to disappear when I start paying off bills, credit cards, loans, etc. The first check I write is to Marin for all the money she loaned me over the years, and the money used to buy out Stan in the divorce. Then I pay off those absurd loans for the checks the lending companies send in the mail, pay the credit cards off online, and I put ten thousand in each kid's five twenty-nine Plan accounts. I feel like it is my responsibility as a mother to at least try to help them pay for some for their college funds. I am left with just about thirty thousand to put in savings. It is pathetic to think I have been working hard since I was a teenager and all I am worth is a measly thirty thousand dollars.

Making the move across the highway feels good. It feels good to be out of the neighborhood and to know I am now living away from Jim, Louanne and Doug Hibben.

Fall is in the air and October is one of my favorite months in Wilmington because it is not too hot, not humid and the average temperatures is six-six degrees. I come home early on this Thursday afternoon and I am sitting on the front porch with a glass of Cabernet. I sometimes like drinking red wine in the fall and winter.

My iPhone rings: Jason is calling; "Bad news, I had the hearing with the judge today for filing the third- party suit against Louanne. Jim's attorney Fred did a good job and said it would be badgering the witness. Unfortunately, Jim's lawsuit against you will move forward. After Louanne lied in her deposition, I think we need to now subpoena depositions from everyone; Pastor Rick and Libba Dennis and the hospice nurse, Shirley Harvey. I want to know in advance what their story will be versus being surprised at their testimony in a courtroom'. Tears start running down my face and I just feel numb and stop listening as he instructs me to get rid of any money I have left for the sale of my home; hide it somewhere, put in my daughter's account, or give to Marin to keep.

My next session with Meg was the usual, expressing anger at my mother. How do you forgive a dead person? "I believe that it would have been easier being raped, left naked on the side of the road to die, then to be put through this torture of the lawsuit. I feel like the church is raping me, trying to take my home away from me by supporting Jim." The bible instructs us that we are to forgive those that persecute us, but I never expected to be persecuted by a church. Basically, whatever the outcome, if there is any money taken from me that goes to the church, those hypocrites and the church are guilty of the equivalent of rape in my mind. They are trying to rape money from me.

Meg keeps telling me in almost every session that my mom knew I could handle this mess. But I keep telling her the Lord knew I could handle it. Meg sends me an email after this week's session.

October 21, 2017 at 7:09 PM Meg Talbot wrote: meg@seagatecounseling.com

> Scarlet,
> I noticed how angry you felt today that no one else seems to get how much you resent the predicament your mother and the circumstances of her death put you in. A strong independent woman like yourself, I suppose, would be even more dumbfounded by how your mom could have let this happen. You felt this way initially when she died, and it makes sense to still feel this way especially after putting your grief/loss on hold dealing with the events of the trial. Several things keep bringing back your frustrations reminding you of how convinced your mom was that she was helpless. From my point of view, she did not have near the strength that you do. She could not protect herself, nor you from what was to come. She gave in like countless victims of emotional and physical abuse do. In hindsight, I could see you rising above and being her strength for her if possible. Try to let 'hindsight' lead you away from resentment and continuing to be the strength for your children.
>
> I really think your dad's positive presence can help as well too, not just for you but also for Samantha and

Sheldon. Marin might also benefit from the 'wake-up call' of how hard it is for you to not see your mother in the same light as her.

I've attached something I copied about the anger phase of grief that may be helpful for you to read again. Your grief has been long and complicated so it's good to be reminded of the process:

After denial, anger is an emotion that has a bad reputation. As you emerge from the state of denial the reality and the pain of your loss will be felt and you might not be ready for it. When intense emotions surface and we feel vulnerable, it's only natural to express these feelings as anger.

The anger may be aimed at complete strangers, friends and family, or the world in general. It may be directed at our dying or deceased loved one. Of course, deep down we know that no one or thing can be blamed for our loss. Emotionally, however, we're not so pragmatic.

Anger is a necessary stage of the healing process and you must be willing to feel your anger, even it seems wrong or limitless. Underneath anger is your pain.

You might feel deserted and abandoned, but you can actually find strength in anger. It can be an anchor, giving you temporary structure while you feel the emptiness of loss. When we loss someone we are lost at sea – embrace your anger as a life-raft and over time it will dissipate and you'll suddenly find yourself ashore.

Meg

I get up from reading that email, and I find all my photo albums in a cardboard box in the back of the coat closet. One by one, I go through each page and pull out every picture that has mom in it; from my birth though adulthood. I realize how few pictures I have of mom compared to those I have of dad and dad's family. I feel like burning them all but decide against that method. I then rip up every picture of her, rip into shreds with my hands, tearing them in small pieces and then put them in the kitchen trash can. Then I go look in my closet and go through my clothes and pull out any clothing item, pocketbook or pair shoes that mom ever bought me, and I place them by the front door. Then I remember mom gave me the "Jesus Calling' book and I go back to my bedroom and find it in the bedside table. There is a stack of books inside the nightstand and I search through them and find one more book mom gave me about mothers and daughters. I go to the kitchen and place the two books in the trash. Then I load up the clothes and other items and put in the trunk of my car to take to Good Will. Now there is nothing left in my home to remind me of my mother.

∎∎∎

Chapter 20: God's Wrath

March rolls around and spring fever is in the air. Wilmington is so beautiful this time of year. The azaleas are in full bloom. The trial is finally scheduled for the week before Easter to start on Monday, April second. Thankfully, it is spring break week so Marin and Rich will be able to come down for the trial with the boys. Talk about perfect timing. By now I can recite much of the scriptures in The Armor of God book and the apostle Paul has become my favorite biblical character. I literally have read the chapters in this book over and over again for over for months now. I still hope and pray the Lord will intervene with this nightmare.

Jason schedules a meeting in on Wednesday to discuss our preparations for the trial. He thinks the trial will last four days. First, he says he needs another ten thousand dollars upfront before the trial. The total amount for the legal fees is now already up to fifty-three thousand dollars.

I tell Jason that I put a contract on a nice condo and the real estate closing is scheduled for April nineteenth. It is a beautiful property, a two-bedroom, two bath, one thousand square feet unit, and it is closer to the Forden Bridge, less than two miles away. The place looks like Joanna Gaines remodeled it with gray shiplap over the fireplace, black barn doors in both bedrooms and white ones in the dining area, gray walls in the entire unit, white granite in the kitchen with white tile backsplash, upgraded stainless steel appliances, true hardwood floors and tiled baths. I am so excited to be a homeowner again. After paying off my debts from the sale of my house, the thirty thousand dollars savings left was enough for a down payment.

We start planning for trial, what clothes I need to wear and the colors. He suggests a navy-blue dress or a blue pant suit, the typical banker attire. And to wear my pearl necklace. He tells me how he thinks I should style my hair, maybe up in a bun, pulled back to look professional and conservative.

"It's spring break week for New Hanover County Schools, can I have protesters outside the courthouse?' Jason says, 'I like how you think'. I tell him I can get Sheldon and his friends to do it and I will make the signs on poster board in purple and green lettering, since those were mom's favorite colors.

'Justice for Glenna' on some boards and scripture on others.

Hypocrite Scripture; 1 John 4:20 "Whoever claims to love God yet hates a brother or sister is a liar. For whoever does not love their brother and sister, whom they have seen, cannot love God, whom they have not seen." ... For the person who does not love his brother or sister whom he has seen cannot love God whom he has not seen."

Luke 20:46-47
[46] "Beware of the teachers of the law. They like to walk around in flowing robes and love to be greeted with respect in the marketplaces and have the most important seats in the synagogues and the places of honor at banquets. [47] They devour widows' houses and for a show make lengthy prayers. These men will be punished most severely."

'Can I contact the press?' He says "Definitely'. Jason agrees that too is a good idea, to find some news outlet to cover the story. Kate has said all along she keeps waiting for this story to be seen on Inside Edition or Dateline. I am still hopeful that this story will make National headlines at some point.

At the end of the meeting, he is adamant that Marin reaches out to Jim and ask him to drop this frivolous lawsuit. Jason really doesn't want to go to trial and he again says all Jim needs is one juror to believe my email was not true. Jason is worried about the people in the church supporting him and wanting the money from me to divided in half for both churches, CoastalLife Community Church and Seaside Baptist Church.

He states "Sharon will be your most compelling witness, the fact that Jim's own daughter is flying across the country to testify against her father on your behalf, it will be captivating to a jury. Narcissist's can't handle shame. Sharon is the only person that can shame him.' Jason believes we are fully prepared for the trial. He talks about the jury selection process and the type of people he would like on the jury; single moms, someone who has lost a mother, and a mixture of people that are religious and some that aren't.

My other witnesses are mom's closest lifelong true friends; Kate Mulvaney, Bethany Miller, Greg Girdwood, Cathy Hillrom and Kathy Denlinger, and the Hospice nurse Shirley. I reserve an Airbnb house for the week in downtown Wilmington large enough for them all to stay in and it conveniently located three blocks for the New Hanover County Courthouse. Mom's best friend Bethany has been in out of ICU with obstructed bowels and she comes out of ICU each time asking the doctor if she will live long enough to make it until the trial. She can't drive so I am going to have to drive to Raleigh on Sunday to get her and bring her back to Wilmington and then take her back to after the trial is over. At least it is not too far of a drive, a little over two hours one way. Bethany has never liked and Jim and says he was always a controlling jerk.

Sharon calls to give me her flight schedule from Los Angeles and George will be traveling with her. She tells me how nervous she is as she never wants to lay eyes on her dad ever again. She went to the doctor to get a prescription for Xanax to help her get through this trial. I start to perceive just how troublesome this trial is for everyone. Sharon still can't believe this is happening and as a non-believer she doesn't understand why anyone could call themselves a Christian and support Jim. 'Scarlet, would the church actual take money from you, take your home from you?" I reply 'They already have. The bible says the thought of sin is sin. They are all hoping to get any amount of money from me from this lawsuit for the sake of the church finances.' Sharon still says she doesn't understand why her dad didn't believe mom was going to die, she asks "Isn't dying part of your faith? Believing that you will die and go to heaven.' And I say 'yes, that is our prize, that is what we live for, death is our reward, as we get to live again forever in heaven with Jesus'. She said 'well, then, why doesn't my dad understand that?' and I respond, 'that's a very good question'.

'What is hardest for me though, is mom's church friends that are supporting him, especially Lindsey Lawton. She is on Jim's witness list. Mom had multiple conversations with her about how worried she was about the Will and how Jim would treat me after he passed, because Jim is so difficult to get along with. I guess mom can see from heaven now who her true friends are, those who are supporting me. Sad thing is I can forgive Jim, because he really isn't a true Christian and has never had the Lord in his heart. But the hypocrites that were born and raised in a church their whole lives, mom's church friends that claim to be true Christian, I don't know how I can ever forgive them for indirectly trying to make me homeless.' Sharon says she can't wait until this is over. But she says that she does look forward to seeing me and Marin though.

Marin and Rich had to cancel their vacation in the Dominican Republic to fly to Wilmington for the trial. It is the annual Horace Mann School spring break trip and both Larry and Bill are so disappointed they aren't able to go. Bill has some insight asking Marin, 'Mom, was Jim always mean to grandma and we just never realized it'? Children can be so perceptive and are smarter than most adults give them credit for. I think everyone is starting to understand how much abuse my mom might have endured during her twenty-six years marriage to this man.

Before I get in bed tonight, I look in the bathroom mirror and recognize the stress the past two and half years has aged me, gaining all my weight back, more gray hair, wrinkles on my face. The sleepless nights, the anger, the fear of losing everything.

Suddenly, it hits me that this ordeal is a huge burden to others too and I am overcome with anxiety. All these people traveling to support me. And poor Sharon, that fact that she has to face her father in a court of law. I make a firm decision that I must put an end to this nightmare, I decide I will call Jason tomorrow.

'I cannot go through with this, I cannot ask these people supporting me to go through this, I will stand before the church and apologize, I will sign a confession judgement, I will do whatever it takes to make this all go away'. Jason has advised against the confession judgement from the beginning, but this is the one solution I can think of to make it all go away for everyone. Jason explains that if I sign the confession judgment, and because I am no longer worth one hundred thousand dollars in equity, then once my new condo has that amount in equity in the future, Jim's heirs can come after my property which means my uncle Daniel can take the home from me at that point in time. He continues to babble with his legal jargon.

'SECTION 15-41-30. Property exempt from attachment, levy, and sale.

> Anything you do specifically to protect the condo from a judgement creditor can and likely would/will be unraveled. The best course of action is to not purchase any property in your name and to, instead, shelter any funds in retirement accounts. If you insist on purchasing the property, it would be best to have someone else purchase it and to rent it from them. Of course, none of this will matter if you are victorious at trial. '

Jason will call Fred to see if Jim would accept a formal public apology as a solution to a settlement.
Jason calls back within the hour, that didn't take long, but Fred says Jim will not accept an apology because most of the people in the church are supporting him anyway. But that also helps my case, because Jim has not really suffered any damage from my supposedly slanderous email. He hasn't lost anything.

Jason again is demanding that Marin reach out to Jim and ask him to drop the case, since she refused to do so from his last request. I call Marin one more time to ask her to contact Jim and she says she is very hesitant to do so because she does not think it will work, but okay then, she will do it.

In a message dated 3/26/2018 6:31:00 PM Eastern Standard Time, Marin Oakley <marin69@gmail.com> writes:

Subject: My Mom

Jim,

I know you don't want to hear from me since I paid for Scarlet's legal defense in your lawsuit against her. I have no doubt that is what Mom would have wanted me to do in order to protect her daughter and grandchildren from your lawsuit against her seeking money. Mom would also want me to reach out to you to make sure you understand what you are about to bring on yourself, my Mom, her grandchildren, and her friends at the trial. Everyone already saw the email that Scarlet sent to the Sunday school class that you are basing your entire lawsuit against her on. Because you are suing her, witnesses will be forced to publicly share at trial those many negative facts. I hope you understand that is what will be happening at your lawsuit trial against Scarlet. My Mom does not deserve this negativity that will become public all because you want money from Scarlet that she doesn't have so is not possible to ever get.

Remember my mom telling you she "would haunt you from my grave" if you did anything negative towards the Gaines family? My mom shared many things with me as well as with her lifelong friends. Remember when she was crying every day, not over cancer but because she was worried about what you would do to the Gaines family after she was gone? Everyone is going to learn that Mom's grandchildren are so poor they are on Medicaid, yet you are suing her for money she doesn't have and will never get, regardless of the trial outcome, and causing her huge legal fees in order to defend the lawsuit against her. My own children keep asking when are we ever going to see Jim again, when are we spending Christmas with Jim again. Children do not know the difference between step grandparents and blood related grandparents. I had to tell my kids who were 9 years old. and 11 years old at the time, that their beloved step Grandfather Jim is suing their Grandmother's daughter for money.

I'm very sorry if you think I had any knowledge of her ever planning to send an email like that. I certainly did not have any knowledge of that. Not that I have any control over her actions anyway, but it was a big surprise to me, just like it was to you. Of course, I wish she would have never sent that email. The same way I wish you would not have disowned her and her children several days after my mom died.

I hope you will ask yourself what your wife would want you to do in this situation. Your wife that told me she told you "I will haunt you from my grave if you do anything negative to the Gaines family". Don't listen to those around you that are benefitting from you financially or hope to one day. I know you know I do not need or want a dollar from you so I have no reason to share this with you other than being the voice for my mother. She told me things so I could be her voice in this situation that she feared before her death. Please ask yourself if my mother deserves all of this negativity to be brought out to the public. Please ask yourself why she was crying in those final weeks about her fears about what you would do after she died and why she felt the need to tell you "I will haunt you from my grave".

You can hate the Gaines family for the rest of your life but I think you should seriously consider dropping your lawsuit against Scarlet as a way to show respect for my mom, your wife. She would not want her own daughter and grandchildren to continue to suffer. I just ask that you consider what you think my mom, your wife, would want you to do and to not be influenced by those around you.

I truly hope you find healing and peace regardless of your decision. At the very least, please pray about what you think my Mom would want you to do.

Sincerely,
Marin

From: **Jim Reardon** <reardonjg@gmail.com>
Date: Mon, Mar 26, 2018 at 7:58 PM
Subject: Re: My Mom
To: marin69@aol.com

Marin,

This has NEVER been about money. Why don't you ask Scarlet where she was the several days before her mother's passing, then she showed up at noon the day that her mother passed away. She did NOT care about your mother, the only thing that she cared about was the money that your mother spent on HER!

How many times did Scarlet visit?

What I want to see at the trial is for 12 people in the jury to themselves see what a terrible daughter that Glenna left on this earth. Nothing more and nothing less, not about money. The Lord has blessed me with enough money to last me for the few remaining years that I have left before I join Glenna, as I approach 83.

Glenna is crying out but, not for the same reason that YOU and SCARLET thinks that she is. Glenna knows that I would not drag or harm her in ANY way. Glenna knows that I LOVED her more than life. And, for Scarlet to say otherwise is absolutely ridiculous!
In ending, It appears as though I will see you in court.
Jim

Jason calls in the morning elated because Jim said that 'this has never been about the money and it is about twelve jurors realizing what a terrible daughter Scarlet was to her mother'. Yet, he is suing me for money, and he says it is not about the money.' Jason forwards the email to Jim's attorney, Fred Casey. Fred calls Jason and says, 'this case is getting nuttier each month'. Jason replies 'Fred, it's been nutty since day one'. Now Fred finally admits that he can't take this case to trial. He asks Jason for me to come up with a one hundred thousand cash settlement (knowing Marin and Rich have that kind of money and they are most likely going to bail me out). Marin says 'no, ten thousand is the final offer'.

Jason calls Fred and they agree on the ten thousand because at this point, Fred knows if it goes to trial, Jim will get nothing, and the judge will probably dismiss the case. Marin overnights the ten-thousand dollars settlement check via overnight mail to Jason's office. I feel relieved this is all over and I can go on with my life. Relief that this nightmare is over for the people that have supported me, the people willing to testify, those that are true Christians, those willing to stand up for righteousness.

Dad is right, he always is, this whole ordeal has been nothing but an attack on Satan. Dad knew all along the Lord was in control and He would work it out.

■■

It's a crisp cool spring Sunday morning. The church parking lot is full even though it is the week after Easter Sunday and although some people haven't returned from spring break vacations. The azaleas are in full bloom in pink and white surrounding the old brick building.
It's a stereotypical sermon; Pastor Dennis preaches his usual boring mundane Southern Baptist message. It's near the end of the service, the choir stands and sings while the offering plates are being passed around each pew by the Deacons.

Jim puts a ten-thousand dollars check in the offering plate. He immediately falls to his death on the red-carpet floor.

Romans 12:17-19 New King James Version (NKJV)

Repay no one evil for evil. Have regard for good things in the sight of all men. If it is possible, as much as depends on you, live peaceably with all men. Beloved, do not avenge yourselves, but rather give place to wrath; for it is written, "Vengeance is Mine, I will repay," says the Lord.

A portion of the proceeds from the sale of this book will be donated to the National Coalition Against Domestic Violence.

Made in the USA
Columbia, SC
07 February 2021